Wilderness Cry

To Greg
Love, Prov, Joy

[signature]

Wilderness Cry

A SCIENTIFIC AND PHILOSOPHICAL
APPROACH TO UNDERSTANDING
GOD AND THE UNIVERSE

Hilary L. Hunt M.D.

Second Edition
Most Chapters Expanded
Two New Chapters

Copyright Registration # TXu 2-017-685
Copyright ISBN- 0000TXU0020176850201
Effective Date of Registration: August 22, 2016

Email: handg@comcast.net

Copyright © 2016 Hilary L. Hunt M.D.
All rights reserved.

ISBN-13: 9781541339576
ISBN-10: 1541339576

About the Author

HILARY LEO HUNT WAS BORN fifth of six boys, deep in the Bible belt, near the small 100 percent Catholic community of Fancy Farm in extreme West Kentucky. I was raised on a very small farm in a three room house with no electricity nor indoor facilities of any kind. Deep in the heart of the Great Depression, from 1933 until 1950, my parents could not afford the cost of having electric lines installed out our narrow private dirt road of nearly one half mile in length. Consequently, all of our studying and other night time activities were done by light from a kerosene lamp. The Illinois Central freight line ran through our front yard; so we were, literally, raised in a three room shack by a railroad track.

We lived a true pioneer life; wood heater stove in the middle of our family room floor and a wood cook stove in the kitchen. We drew water from a deep cistern.

The largest and most prominent building in our community was St. Jerome Catholic church, which still occupies that status today. The school building which is now on the National Registry of Historic Sites housed all twelve grades. All students, except for an occasional non catholic, were required to attend daily Mass, and the first class each day was Catholic Catechism. We were disciplined vigorously in Catholic Religion and it was taught with the same degree of authenticity and certainty as arithmetic and chemistry.

In spite of all adversity, I emerged valedictorian of my small high school graduating class, and that accomplishment earned me a partial scholastic scholarship to Saint Edward's University, Austin, Texas. That school, being operated by the Holy Cross Brothers, was facetiously known as "The Notre Dame of The South". My pre-medical advisor and biology professor was Brother Raphael Wilson of "The Bubble Boy" fame. He was instrumental in getting me accepted into Saint Louis University School of Medicine from where I successfully graduated M.D. in 1958. After completing an internship at St Louis City Hospital and one year of general surgery residency at St Louis County Hospital, I returned to a nearby town of Mayfield, Kentucky, to do Family Practice. After two years of Family Practice I was extremely fortunate to be accepted into the prestigious Campbell Clinic in Memphis, Tennessee for Orthopedic Surgery training. After completing that three year program and passing my preliminary board examination, I was allowed to complete two years of orthopedic practice in Mayfield before being drafted into the U.S. Army during the height of the Vietnam War. While serving as Chief of the orthopedic service at Fort Campbell Kentucky, I was awarded one of the highest non-combat medal the U.S. Army offers, The Meritorious Service Medal. After serving my obligatory two year stint of service and achieving rank of Lieutenant Colonel, I returned to Paducah, Kentucky where I practiced until retirement.

Our first child was born in 1956, between my first and second years of medical school, and our fifth and last child was born in 1968 at Fort Campbell.

My hobbies have always been gardening, hunting, and, in post war years, golf. In addition to high school basketball, I played high school, college, and semi-pro baseball. My first sports love was St. Louis Cardinals baseball and, of course, Kentucky Wildcat basketball is number one on my list of sports favorites.

Table of Contents

About the Author · v
Dedications · ix
Acknowledgements · xi
Introduction · xiii

Chapter 1	Developing Doubt ·	1
Chapter 2	God and the Trinity ·	5
Chapter 3	The Trinity and Gods Will ·	10
Chapter 4	Creation, Evolution and Gods Will · · · · · · · · · · · · · ·	12
Chapter 5	Sin and Prayer ·	17
Chapter 6	A Prescription for Success ·	23
Chapter 7	The Bible ·	24
Chapter 8	The Unholy Triumvirate ·	28
Chapter 9	Evil in the Universe ·	32
Chapter 10	Evolution of evil ·	34
Chapter 11	What About Selfishness? ·	38
Chapter 12	God In the Universe ·	40
Chapter 13	Universality of God ·	43
Chapter 14	The Holy Spirit ·	46
Chapter 15	The Holy Spirit (Will of God) Explained · · · · · · · · · · ·	50
Chapter 16	Omni God ·	53
Chapter 17	God, The Universe and Heaven, Man as God · · · · · · · ·	55
Chapter 18	Eternity ·	57
Chapter 19	But for the Grace of God, There Go I · · · · · · · · · · · · · ·	60

Chapter 20	Jesus (The Christ)	64
Chapter 21	Why Jesus Had to Die	68
Chapter 22	Creeds Versus The Bible	73
Chapter 23	Eucharist	75
Chapter 24	The Soul	77
Chapter 25	Marriage and Sex	80
Chapter 26	Love Versus Mercy	87
Chapter 27	Free Will	90
Chapter 28	Free Will and the Legal System	92
Chapter 29	On Magisterium	95
Chapter 30	Human Nature and Social Experiment	98
Chapter 31	The Future of Christianity	101
	Summary	109
	References	113

Dedications

This work is dedicated to the billions of Christians who, throughout the centuries, have suffered overwhelming guilt, humiliation, torture and death at the hands of organized religion.

Also, it is dedicated to Bro Magellan who taught me Logic at St. Edwards University, Austin, Texas. He impressed upon me the undying fundamental that TRUTH must be sought, accepted, and honored at all cost. It was through his skillful and diligent tutoring that I learned the art and science of right thinking. I shall be forever grateful.

Acknowledgements

THE COMPILATION OF THE MATERIAL and ideas in this thesis has been the result of a fifty year endeavor. It began in earnest when I came to the disheartening realization that the religion in which I had been rigorously inculcated was at best terribly misguided and at worst a complete hoax. I had been taught fifteen years of "factual" religion. The word faith was never mentioned. With the advent of the Second Vatican Council, the word faith came into regular use. At first I ignored it, thinking it an aberration. However, soon enough I came to the startling realization that the religion I had been taught as being factual and irrefutable was really a faith-based system of rules and regulations which had been developed and changed, ad nauseam, throughout the centuries. As a scientist, I had learned that little, if anything, of absolute nature could be accepted without proof. That guiding principle forced me to seek the TRUTH at all cost.

That endeavor brought immense anguish and concern to my wife, Ginny, who, like me, was raised a devout Catholic. I cannot thank her enough for her tolerance and indulgence.

I am most grateful to my dear friend Donna Morse, who has been my "sounding board" throughout this process. She endured innumerable hours of reading, re-reading and discussion of my writings. Her suggestions, input and encouragement are immeasurable.

I wish to thank with all my heart a local cleric of status who took the time and energy to review and discuss this work with me. While he is truly duty bound to his state in life, he offered me sound assurance that he could find no factual, philosophical, or logical fault in my writings; very hearting, indeed.

Last but not least, I am deeply indebted to my dear daughter-in-law, Lindsey French Mangino, for her untiring and timeless effort in retyping and arranging these writings into proper form for publication.

Introduction

§

ONE MIGHT REASONABLY ASK; WHY this title? What does it mean? Allow me to explain. Ever since I reached the *age of reason*, I have been bombarded with a conglomerate of doctrinal teachings, which, to say the least, have been perplexing, astonishing, at times totally unreasonable, and ultimately unbelievable. In the beginning, I accepted those teachings as absolute truth because I was told that they were indeed absolute, factual and irrefutable. If I, or any others, refused to believe, we would be condemned to hell for all eternity. As I matured physically and rationally, I began to question many of those doctrinal concepts, and by age 30 or so, I decided to embark on a *journey of understanding*. That journey would lead me to a comprehensive reading and re-reading of the bible. Those readings, in turn, immediately created great consternation for me about many things, not the least of which was the very nature of God, Himself. As I began an in depth attempt at conceptualizing God, I was immediately confronted with the *mystery* of the Trinity. That, in turn, led to the development of concepts about God's Will and the Holy Spirit. All of those will be covered in detail in following chapters.

Later on, utilizing my limited background in mathematics, physics, chemistry, biology, and quantum mechanics, in addition to studying the writings of Stephen Hawking and others, I developed a scheme of creation based on the *big bang* which explains precisely the concept of God as Omni-everything (all knowing, all powerful, all loving, all-perfect). It easily explains the perfect universe in which we live; God's one creation and it's continuing chain reaction which some call evolution, the Holy Spirit which is synonymous with God's Will, the true meaning of the Last Supper, the real definition of sin, the relationship of the material universe, including all living and inanimate, to God, and many more concepts which I will develop. On the other hand, my research and study left one immense void; certain knowledge and understanding of and about Jesus Christ. Who is or was Jesus the Christ???

In my opinion, it is impossible to know Jesus from reading the biblical accounts of Him. It seems certain that He did exist and that He was crucified. From there the biblical stories become muddled and contradictory. The earliest writer, Paul believed that Jesus was the Son of God, sent to be tortured and crucified to the death as atonement for our sins. He taught that faith in Jesus was all that was necessary for salvation. Paul claimed to have been given this information directly from God after experiencing some overwhelming reaction while riding to persecute Christians. Paul claims to have received the information without directly encountering either Jesus or the apostles. He freely describes this experience as being possibly metaphysical (not knowing whether he was 'in the body or out of the body"). Paul was convinced that after Jesus ascension into heaven, He was coming back immediately to establish an earthly paradise. Paul's conviction was so strong that in one of his letters, he exhorted the believers to abandon their usual lifestyle of marriage, work, etc. and put on a "holy face", inwardly and outwardly, in preparation for Jesus return.

Later writers had varying opinions of Jesus' real identity; what his death, resurrection and ascension meant, and they disagreed with Paul about requirements for salvation. They seemed to think of Him as the Christ or Messiah, that is the "Chosen One", or messenger, of God, but not God; decades later John's followers wrote that Jesus was Devine; God, but not equal to the Father. In Mark and Matthew Jesus is quoted as saying the Father knows things which He does not. It was 3-4 centuries before the concepts of Jesus similar to what are taught today were developed (Apostles Creed and Nicene Creed). It is my voice that cries loudly and unceasingly for Truth. I am lost in a *Wilderness* of disinformation, misinformation, half-truths and organizational dominance of my life. This treatise is my attempt to disentangle myself from that web of irrationality and make some purposeful sense of my existence. My *hope and trust* is that this book will provoke meaningful thought, research and dialogue among brave thinkers.

CHAPTER 1

Developing Doubt

It was a bright, warm May morning that I and my fellow first-communicants began assembling on the grounds of St. Jerome school. I was a timid tyke, somewhat fearful of approaching events and contemplating what it would be like taking Jesus into my mouth and attempting to swallow Him without chewing. I had been well schooled in the sacrilege it would be to allow my teeth to touch the host; it would be mortally sinful to do so deliberately, and moderately sinful to do so accidentally. As I stood alone pondering the consequences of such a breech, suddenly a nun (Sister of Charity), who not only taught us Roman Catholic religion but all our other subjects in school, came rushing up to the nearby open-faced water fountain and hastily, securely tied a cloth over the fountain, so that we could not accidentally, forgetfully, take a sip of water. If any one of us had done so, we would not have been allowed to make out first communion; deliberately receiving Holy Communion after eating or drinking anything after midnight was a *mortal* sin and would mean certain and direct condemnation to hell for all eternity if one died before confessing that sin. What a terrifying thought!!! I was seven years old at the time, and literally believed what I was told.

Later in life, after multiple changes in directives regarding taking Communion (nowadays, most communion hosts are distributed by lay people and the recipient not only takes it into his/her hand but is also encouraged to chew the host vigorously as though eating real food), I now realize that what I had perceived at age seven to be a God given directive mediated through the church to be nothing more than someone's (hierarchy of the church) made up rule under the guise of *Magisterium* (the teaching authority of the church). That realization made me angry as did rules about eating meat on Friday and days of lent, only to have them changed and nearly abolished, to more recently having them partially reinstated; (*the hierarchy seem to be to be having a difficult time reading God's mind or God keeps changing His mind; I doubt that*). If I sound cynical, you read correctly. The same is true about so many rules of the church. When I was young, before the second Vatican council, priests presided at mass with their backs to the congregation and said the mass prayers in LATIN; now they face the congregation and read the mass in native tongue. Most Catholic churches have kneelers but some don't; how come? Does it really matter?

At age 22, I was fortunate enough to marry the woman of my dreams. She was the strength of my life and mother of our five children. I was in medical school, penniless, and soon with a pregnant wife. Artificial birth control was out of the question. It seemed like Sunday after Sunday the pulpits riled against artificial birth control, and year after year, more babies appeared that scarcely could be cared for. We were able, by enduring unbelievable torment, hardship and sacrifice, to get our children grown, educated and self-reliant. I wouldn't trade the world for any one of them, but I have often thought of how much less traumatic it would have been if a little *family planning* had been allowed.

I can't recall a single mention of artificial birth control from any pulpit within the last 20 years, or so. This angers and frustrates me because I suspect it has become *politically incorrect* and potentially *economically unwise* to do otherwise. In the meantime, it seems morality can and does take a *back-seat* to money, power and control. It is obvious, from simple observation, and casual conversation with young people, that artificial family planning is the norm among Catholics rather than the exception. Ranting and raving about artificial family planning would fall mostly on *deaf ears* and, possibly, would anger many to the point of leaving the church or, more importantly, reducing or eliminating financial support.

At about the time our last child was born, I began searching desperately for answers. I began to wonder if the church really did have the answers. My first approach was the bible; I read the Old Testament cover to cover and then the New Testament. The most striking thing I encountered in the old testament, outside of the immediate discrepancy of the creation story in Genesis 1 and 2, was the portrayal of God, Himself. I had been taught that God created me equal to every other human and that he loved me equally as others, even to having His Son die for me. But in the Old Testament, God is repeatedly described as a string-pulling puppeteer, who is manipulative and vengeful, and readily willing to slaughter millions of his own people on a whim. The Old Testament God could be *influenced* to the point of changing HIS mind. Throughout my lifetime, that characterization of God persists in the Catholic Church. We are led to believe that God's mind can be changed; that by relentless petitioning by both the living and the dead, somehow, God can be dissuaded from levying hurt on us. Additionally, it is commonly believed that by continuous begging and relentless repetition, God can be influenced to do something: i.e.; make it rain, cure an illness, etc. As I contemplated that philosophy concerning God, I soon concluded that I did not know such a God. My God was perfect and unchangeable in every respect. When I confronted my pastor with that observation he said to me, "most people don't think that deeply". And my response, "what does that have to do with anything?" No answer. I then began to analyze my understanding of God as Omni-everything. That analysis will be presented in a later chapter.

That concept of God immediately brings into question the subject of prayer; what is its purpose and how should it be directed; a discussion for another chapter. Also, the concept of God as Omnipresent augments my concepts of creation, the Trinity, and the Last Supper; other chapters.

With the advent of the personal computer and the internet, I had instant access to, heretofore, difficult to obtain church history. As I read and studied, I was shocked and appalled by the hideous crimes committed, in the name of God, by the Church. Early on, the suppression of legitimate religious practices; later, the buying and selling of indulgences; the inquisition; the burning at the stake of innocent people, some of whom were children, as witches; the terrorizing and house arrest of Galileo because of his scientific discovery of the solar system, *refuting the churches notion that the earth was the center of the universe*; the relentless slaughter of the descendants of Ishmael during the crusades, some of which were led by popes themselves; and the list goes on and on.

Throughout my entire life I have witnessed the utter and complete failure of the church. Instead of bringing a message of *understanding and acceptance* of God's Will, the church has continuously and continually promulgated a religion of *guilt and suppression* (get down on your knees, you worthless piece of scum); you are worthless but if you beg hard enough (what is enough?), I will forgive your sins. The power is mine, says the Church. I have witnessed the making of innumerable *basket cases* generated in guilt ridden religious fanatics.

Our preachers should be bringing a message of knowledge and understanding of *the love of God* based on HIS LOVE as demonstrated by His perfection; I will explain later. They should be teaching a thorough graphic understanding of the Trinity and Its function instead of making it a so called *mystery* which is unknowable: I will give you that understanding. They should teach us how to pray and what to expect from prayer rather than the mythology promulgated now. They should teach us the real meaning of Jesus' words at the last supper; I will give you a concrete opinion based on both philosophical and scientific considerations.

Then there is the subject of intellect and will. I will submit to you there is no such thing as *free will*, and I will draw that subject out later. As I write this treatise, I have no doubt that I will be attacked from all sides. However, I would rather endure the attacks tenfold than shirk my duty by not sharing my thoughts with you. You may say: "WHO ARE YOU TO BE MAKING SUCH BOLD AND OUTRAGEOUS STATEMENTS?" And I answer; "I AM ONE CRYING OUT FOR TRUTH FROM A WILDERNESS OF CONFUSION, MISCONCEPTION, DECEIT, IGNORANCE, AND INTOLERANCE."

CHAPTER 2

God and the Trinity

ANY DISCUSSION OF GOD WOULD assume that He (She-It) exists. While there are some, maybe many, who do not accept the existence of God, I do believe, without reservation, that there is a God, and based on my observations and understandings of the natural universe, I have ascribed certain characteristics to Him. I will describe a few in detail to emphasize the points. It should be noted here that no one, as far as I can determine, has ever seen God. Throughout the ages, including Old Testament times, there are numerous instances of people hearing God's voice; many times the voice addresses a random audience, and at other times God's voice speaks directly to individuals. Instances of God speaking to people in dreams are described in various places. In modern times people who hear voices are generally thought of as hallucinating because of an emotional and/or mental aberration. As a physician, I have encountered many people who either claimed to be God or to have the power of God, or to be acting on orders from God. Without exception, those people were classified as individuals who had lost contact with reality (become insane [psychotic]). Also there have been descriptions and assertions, by many individuals, of visions of various religious figures, most notably the Virgin Mary. Whether or not those visions represented actual *physical* events or were simply *visual hallucinations*, I cannot say for certain; however I suspect the latter.

My understanding of God is based primarily on what I have observed and learned about His creation.

1. God is perfect in every respect:
    a. Something that is perfect, by its very nature, cannot be changed; is it possible to be more perfect then perfect?
    b. God cannot be please or hurt. Admitting the possibility of such would be admitting to an inherent defect in God's perfection and would completely negate the concept of perfectness. Pleasing him admits to the existence of a *pleasure port* that is insufficiently filled, a partial void, a defect, and certainly not perfect. Hurting him would admit to the existence of *cracks in His armor* where noxious agents could penetrate and cause damage, eliminating His perfection.
    c. I base my understanding of God on my observation of His universe: *everything* and *every occurrence* in this universe is perfect. There is absolutely nothing nor any occurrence, nor has there ever been, that is not a perfect example of what it is. Allow me to explain. If I were to throw an ordinary glass tumbler against a brick fireplace, the glass would shatter into many pieces of varying size and shape, and the pieces would be spread out in random pattern in the vicinity. The exact number of pieces, their exact dimension and their exact location would be the perfect result of many foregoing consequences; i.e.; the exact composition, size and shape of the glass, the angle at which the glass struck the brick, and the velocity of the glass at moment of impact, just to name a few. If I threw a second glass, the result would be similar but different, because in all likelihood, the multiple consequences leading up to the two events would vary somewhat, and so would the result; however, each result would be perfect for its set of circumstances. So it is in the universe; every instance of every occurrence in this universe since the beginning of time has been perfect and always will be. I say this because of my observation of natural law occurrences. My thesis mandating that conclusion is based on a concept that everything is empowered by the perfect Will of God, the

Holy Spirit. I will elucidate that concept farther in my discussion of the far reaching implications regarding sin, prayer, the Eucharist and more.

2. God is almighty:
    a. We have gained so much knowledge and understanding of the physical universe since biblical and pre-biblical times. During those days, superstition, magic, sorcery, and witchcraft ran rampant. For the most part, people were illiterate, superstitious and very impressionistic. Their concepts of the universe were based only on what they could see and imagine. With no scientific understanding at all, their imaginations ran wild as their resulting superstitious beliefs and practices indicate. Things are different now; scientific understanding, while still very rudimentary, has given us a much clearer picture to consider as we contemplate the serious matters of God and the universe. We know for sure that the earth is not the center of the universe, as was taught and mandated, to the point of execution, by the church for over 1200 years (Magisterium?).
    b. While we know nothing with absolute certainty, as far as I can determine, no one has certain knowledge of a competing God or universe. We have suggestions from our most astute scientists that there may well be a parallel universe or universes. The implications of those possibilities are not fully understood, if at all. It suffices to say that, with our present state of understanding, our God is in total charge and command. When one considers the vastness and magnitude of our universe, *an impossible task of its own*, one would be obliged to accept the almighty power of its creator; don't you think? I might interject that recent observations by the Hubbell telescope indicate that there are more stars (suns) in the universe than there are grains of sand on all of the earth's beaches. That is some imponderable number and considering the fact that suns are known to be millions and even billions of miles apart,

the magnitude of the universe is unimaginable; *and there is a God that created this all and knows and empowers each and every building block (proton, neutron and electron)" of which it is made*; some great big, powerful God eh???

3. God is all knowing:

   When we consider the perfect order and functionality in the universe, and accept the concept of a creator, we are compelled to assume that God knew what he was doing in His process of its' creation. It is impossible to imagine an uncontrolled, disordered universe where no physical element obeyed any physical law. The resultant chaos would be unimaginable. My contention is that God knows each atomic and subatomic particle by name, so to speak, and knows from His empowerment of it exactly what it has done and will do forever. Furthermore, since those creations follow an exact law of operation, their activities and consequences are mathematically predictable: *if only we had Gods mind*. This alludes to a concept of heaven; seeing God as He truly is, *a perfect Rational Being*.

4. God is all good:

   a. Everywhere in the universe Gods *goodness* is visible in His *perfection*. One might ask, as did Bart Ehrman, in his studious and enlightening book, *Jesus Interrupted*, how can God be good and allow so much suffering in the world. That question begs of the very concept of God's nature, and more importantly, *how man throughout the ages has interpreted* God's nature. My contention is that mankind, for the most part, has tried to *humanize* God. Man's ego has allowed him to see himself as set apart from the rest of God's creation, and become something *special* in "God's eye". Some people throughout history have even gone so far as to believe and state emphatically that they were the "chosen" people of God to the abandonment of the rest of the human race. In the Catholic consecration prayer those words are ritually spoken at every mass; "From age to age, You gather a people unto Yourself, so that from east to west a perfect offering may be made --". My concept is that Homo sapiens *is just one more step* in Gods *ongoing creation*. As such we are subject to the same perfection in God's universe as all other living and non-living things. That is not to say that God holds us in any form of disregard; it simply means that we must be willing to *accept our place*, with its trials and tribulations, in this universe just as all other existences. God in His infinite Wisdom and Goodness gave us a rationality to deal with it. Some things we do are beneficial and others not. I submit that our goal is basically summed up in the *Serenity Prayer*; oh God give me the serenity to accept the things I cannot change, the courage to change the things I can, and the wisdom to know the difference. I believe everything in this universe is SPECIAL but nothing is more special to God; to be so would indicate a *weakness* in His armor.

5. There are many other attributes of God but they are basically contained in the above concepts.

CHAPTER 3

The Trinity and Gods Will

§

ALL OF MY RATIONAL LIFE, I have listened to preachers expound about the Trinity, only to admit that it is a mystery and not understandable for us mere mortals. The same can be said of God's Will. I have listened to seemingly endless tongue wagging about God's will, but never even once have I heard a suitable description. Just recently, I heard a young priest defy anyone to *attempt to know or define* God's will. Yet in the very next breath, he bombarded us with exhortations to *do God's will*. Will someone please, please, please explain to this simpleton how it is possible to properly accomplish anything without *knowledge and understanding* of the stated task?

I have answers for both; they fit together like a hand in a glove, and are inseparable; let us start. They have as their basis a *definition of God*.

1. God is a perfect rational being:
    a. What are the attributes of a rational being? Simply stated, they are two; an Intellect which *perceives*, and a Will which *achieves*.
    b. If we think of God as a Perfect Intellect, then we must ask the question; what would a Perfect Intellect Perceive, *reflect upon, reason about*? The logical answer would be *something perfect*. The only perfect thing in existence is Itself; so this Perfect Intellect reflects upon Itself, and what does it see? It sees Itself; a mirror image if you will, exact and perfect in all respects. Since we are speaking of the supernatural, both of those *Persons* are living; one God; two Persons. For the want of

better terms and because we live in a Patristic society, we call those Persons the Father and the Son; we could say Mother and Daughter; how about It and Itself.

c. What do you suppose happens when two perfect intellects view each other? They do what comes naturally (supernaturally); instantly they *love* what they see; they *choose* each other; they *will* to accept each other. That spiritual flow of intellectual energy between the two; the choosing, the loving, the willing of each other, we call the Holy Spirit, the WILL OF GOD. Since this flow of spiritual energy EXISTS IN PERMANENT STATE BETWEEN THE TWO IT CARRIES THE IMPRINT OF THE GENERATING INTELLECTS, and being supernatural becomes the third person of the Trinity. So here we have a simple, easy to visualize, graphic of the Trinity; Three Persons-the same one God.

d. So how then does the Will of God operate in the universe? That discussion will be covered thoroughly in a future chapter.

CHAPTER 4
Creation, Evolution and Gods Will

§

WE HAVE SEEN HISTORICALLY HOW man has concocted superstitious schemes to explain God's workings; i.e.; the various stories of creation in the Bible. While one of those stories can be true, both cannot, and science and common sense experience tends to lend credence to a different method of creation. The development of the so called *Big Bang* theory of creation generated an instantaneous "big bang" of its own among the fundamentalists (those who believe every word of the bible to be inerrant and to be taken literally). The problem arises when one encounters the multiple discrediting problems with the bible; namely the multiple contradictions, the totally unreasonable statements, such as " you can take up poisonous snakes and drink poison with no harm" (paraphrased), but more importantly, according to Ehrman, less than 1/3 of the new testament was written by the stated author. As far as I can determine, Jesus never wrote a word. What we know or don't know was written years after his death by people who never saw Jesus (Matthew and possibly John the exceptions). At any rate the stir occurred and isn't about to go away. The Big Bang theory lends itself nicely to the concept of one instantaneous creation of all the matter in the universe. What has eventuated after that is what I call *continuing creation*; others call *evolution*.

Knowledgeable scientists tell us that at some point in time, roughly 13.7 billion years ago, all the matter in the universe appeared from a spot no larger than a pin head. That spot is known as *the singularity*. Initially, it was amorphous primordial (primitive building block, which now seem to be recognized as energy quanta with names such as quarks and bosons) material that rapidly formed into the perfect building blocks of all the universe. Those perfect little particles were given the names of 1-neutrons with no electrical charge, 2- identically sized and weighted positively charged particles we call protons, and 3- infinitesimally small negatively charged particles called electrons. There are also energy quanta called photons and other energies, but for our discussion, the three afore mentioned PNE's (protons, neutrons, electrons) will suffice. The protons and neutrons combined in various number combinations to become the atoms of the various elements in the universe. The electrons rotate about this proton-neutron nucleus in varying numbers lesser than or greater than the number of protons to give the atom a resultant net positive or negative charge. Those atoms then combine (react) with each other to form molecules and molecules react with each other to form compounds of varying types. Compounds can amalgamate to form all sorts of materials and substances. Under controlled conditions, use of this knowledge combined with our certainty of the outcome (repeated experimentation has shown us that [science]) is one of the billions of ways Gods perfection and goodness is demonstrated. We are able to produce order out of seeming chaos for the betterment of mankind, and produce goods and products that make us feel better, and make our lives more comfortable. Were those particles not uniform and perfect in every way, we would not be able to deal with them, and the likelihood is that neither we, nor anything else in this universe, to which we are accustomed, would exist.

After the initial chemical reactions began, the energy release was inestimable. The massive outward explosive effect generated the physical resultant of repeated reactions and collisions of particles causing nuclear reactions of unimaginable proportion resulting in the production of heat and light. Massive gas clouds which became *star nurseries* were formed. The massive gas clouds condensed and began to form stars and so a solar system was born. Those systems aggregated into massive organized units called galaxies; and ultimately, the universe was filled with billions of galaxies each containing billions of stars and planets. Gravitational forces in the center of some stars was so great that hydrogen atoms were forced to fuse with each other in varying numbers to form nuclei of all the heavier elements. Exploding stars are given credit for delivering all the heavy elements in the universe today. I realize that this is a gross oversimplification of the Big Bang theory but it will suffice for our purposes here.

The point I am getting to is this. The universe as, we know it, seems to be perfectly organized and functioning properly. That is not to say nor imply that catastrophic events will not happen; just the contrary, they will; they always have and they always will, and always in perfect fashion. The reason is clear, God's Will (the Holy Spirit). Allow me to explain.

Mankind has always interpreted catastrophic events as evidence of God's wrath. He has failed to recognize God's presence in all things and all events. He has failed to see God's continuing creation which generates those events. My model envisions a perfect, all knowing, all powerful, all good God, Who with His perfect Intellect, envisioned His creation; He converted His massive energy into matter (something mankind cannot do; change matter into energy or change energy into matter), ultimately forming the basic building blocks from which all matter is built (PNE's). He formed each of its' kind identical to the other and He commissioned each of them with His Will (Holy Spirit) to remain perfect and to perform perfectly forever. That they have done and always will do. So, the events we witness in the universe are the direct result of God's Will. Hence, my statement that every occurrence of every existence is and has been perfect and is the direct result of GODS WILL (HOLY SPIRIT). Amen. So the conclusion is obvious; no mystery here; GOD IS IN ALL THINGS AND ALL THINGS ARE IN GOD.

That brings me to the Eucharist, *The Bread of Life- Holy Communion*. I know many will think of me as sacrilegious and heretical; I will admit to the heresy, but not to sacrilege. I am a heretic because I am promoting an idea contrary to Church teaching, but that neither makes me wrong or sacrilegious. I have a different perspective. Allow me to explain. When one reads the gospels, with the knowledge and understanding that Mark wrote the first account and sometime later Matthew and the Luke, one is struck by how Matthew and Luke copy almost verbatim Mark's description of the last supper. In that account Jesus blesses bread and wine, distributes them to the apostles telling them it is His body and blood; the bread of eternal life and the blood of the new covenant. He also instructs them to do likewise in *memory* of HIM. The Catholic Church has taken that literally in the sense that by saying those words at the consecration of the mass the bread and wine are turned, trans-substantially, into the real presence of the body and blood of Jesus.

John you will recall was the beloved disciple who laid his head on Jesus chest at the last supper, and the only apostle to attend his crucifixion. Some sixty years after Jesus death someone writing in John's name completely ignores the Eucharist story. It is unthinkable that John would not have known what Jesus meant at the last supper, and certainly if the Eucharist were meant to be the centerpiece of a 60 year old fledgling religion, John would have told the story very emphatically.

The Catholic Church has put out the spin that John was interested in establishing the Divinity of Jesus. I agree that was a problem because few if any of the earlier writers took that view of Jesus; most thought of him as the Messiah (Christ), that is the messenger or chosen one who was to tell about God but not God himself. He was the deliverer of the Jews; one who was to establish a glorious kingdom here on earth once he returned from heaven. That occurrence was generally accepted as being eminent after Jesus' ascension, particularly preached by Paul. When it did not happen in those early writers lifetime, it became obvious that the timetable was indeterminate. John's writer or writers saw it as necessary to establish the true Divinity of Jesus, thereby making Him God; not merely the bearer of good news about an eminent kingdom to come here on earth, but rather a heavenly kingdom. One must legitimately ask, why, if those earlier writers were truly inspired by God, they did not understand Jesus real identity and His inner Divinity? It is quite strange, also, that this doctrine was not completely and legalistically developed until the 4th and 5th centuries.

I will take this opportunity to make some observations that may escape many of the faithful. As I listen to Sunday homilies concerning the scripture readings for the day, I am struck by the observation that any biblical statement which seems irrational such as "you can take up poisonous snakes and drink poisons without being harmed", (paraphrased), are usually explained away as Jesus speaking metaphorically. The reason seems clear; we know and can prove scientifically that those are erroneous statements. However, if a statement can be neither proved nor disproved, such as "This is My body", the Church always interprets it literally. That is an uncanny convenience tool for promoting self-serving ideas and rituals. I will elaborate on John's understanding of those matters in the chapter entitled Eucharist.

My take is straight forward and simple. I must admit, I do not know for sure who Jesus was; I am accepting His inner being (soul) as God. The last supper story makes sense that way only. My contention is that Jesus was telling the apostles a scientific "trade secret" without giving away the formula. How is that you say? If God made all things, and empowered them with his HOLY SPIRIT (WILL), and all things are in God and God is in all things, then the obvious follows; *that bread and wine already was and always were the "body and blood" of Jesus.* Jesus was simply telling the apostles that fact and asked them to keep that in mind when they ate. I think John understood that fact and made nothing more of it. That explanation makes sense and represents my basic thesis.

CHAPTER 5

Sin and Prayer

WHERE DID THE CONCEPT OF sin come from? I don't know for sure but I strongly suspect that Moses or whoever wrote the first books of the Old Testament developed the concept of a vengeful God. He reasoned that when he and his followers sinned (did things God didn't like), they would reap all sorts of wrath and torment at God's hands. He interpreted prosperity as performing in accordance with God wishes, resulting in heavenly favor. The Israelites developed a sacrificial ritual, whereby animals were killed and burned on wooden racks as an atonement and appeasement of God for their misdeeds. They believed that every aberration in their lives was due to sin. As they extended the distance from their Egyptian captors on the way to the Promised Land, they encountered one obstacle after another; famine, thirst and ultimate despair. They lost "faith" in their God and began to worship idols. Their lifestyle became hedonistic. Consequently, Moses, being a dutiful shepherd, and undoubtedly unable to control his clan, went up on the mountain and "was given" a set of stone tablets with specific directives of conduct for avoiding sin. When he presented them to his tribesmen, they ignored them and laughingly continued their merry (sinful) lifestyle. This, both disheartened and angered Moses because he could clearly see that he had lost control of his tribe. So, being an intuitive man, once more he treks to the mountain and returns with a fresh set of stone directives; only this time he presents them as God's directives with admonitions of impending disaster at God's hand if they are not heeded. The Israelites repented for a while. However, as time went, in an attempt to keep God's favor, they saw it as necessary and desirable to proclaim a complex system of social laws that directed literally every minute aspect of Jewish life. They sinned and of course had to pray incessantly to avoid God's wrath. They assumed that by begging God incessantly, they could influence Him to change His mind and refrain from meeting out punishment.

When Jesus came along, his writers report conflicting stories about his relationship with Judaism. Regardless of how one considers the Jesus factor, the eventual church that won out patterned itself precisely after Jewish ritual. Jesus became the un-bloody sacrificial lamb, instead of a real lamb. Instead of God living in the Arc of the Covenant, he now resided in a gold tabernacle. Until recently no one was allowed to touch Jesus except with a thirsty tongue and an empty stomach. Nowadays, every "Tom, Dick, and Harry" is distributing Jesus' body and blood everywhere. It seems odd to me that the *sacredness* of the Jesus host could have changed so drastically; I didn't think God was really changeable. I should have known better because all my life I have been disciplined to get down on my knees and incessantly beg God to change His mind and not punish me. I have recited countless litanies to the saints and recited innumerable rosaries to the Blessed mother pleading with them to intercede for me and change Gods mind. Mindful that I most certainly would go to purgatory first, if, in fact, I ever made it to heaven, I recited every indulgence bearing prayer a thick prayer missal would hold. I attended special Benediction of the Blessed Sacrament regularly pleading with God to make it rain when our crops were burning up and dying from thirst. I prayed for everything imaginable; and you know what? None of those things ever happened. I was told it was Gods Will and I accepted that. Only I began to question why was I doing all that praying when nothing changed? I came to the conclusion that Gods Will was unchangeable. That thought provoked a complete conversion of understanding; the Jews were wrong; the Christian church was wrong, any church was wrong that believed they could influence God's Will. I decided God's Will is eternal, perpetual, unrelenting and unchanging. So where did that leave me? *It left me with a remarkable sense of relief; I no longer had to be God's judge*; He could make, and already had made, His own judgments from all eternity. So what was I to do? Suddenly it struck me. If Gods Will is unchangeable, then I must do as Jesus is reported to have done in the garden of Gethsemane; "Father, not My will, but Your will be done".

So how then should we pray? Very simply; Father, I am mindful that I am a selfish sinner. Also, I am mindful that You sent Your Son, Jesus, to suffer agony and death that my sins might be forgiven. Without You, I am nothing, but by His death, You gave me value and made me worthy. I thank You, dear God, with all the intellectual energy You bestowed on me, for my life, my sustenance, and my salvation. Amen

That brings me to another topic of consideration, that of free will. This statement will undoubtedly shock many people but I do not accept the concept of free will. Allow me to explain. There really is no such thing as Free Intellect. Certainly we are free to study, learn and cipher. But any conclusions we reach must be based on sound logic in order to be acceptable. It is entirely possible that the premises we accept as true in our logical process may, in fact, be in error, and, therefore, as a result, the logical conclusion we reach will be inherently wrong. That fact, however, does not change the principal that the intellect chooses based on the information at hand. The intellect is free to make judgments, but the conclusions reached are mandated by reason and logic. In that sense the intellect is not free. It is duty bound to judge by logic.

Similarly, the will is not free to operate independently from the intellect; that is, the will is not a free agent. Just as the Will of God is not free to operate independently, the Father and Son see each other as perfectly good; therefore, Their Will's have no choice but to accept each other, so also with the human will. Whatever the intellect presents to the will as good and true (more desirable), the will must choose; it is never free to reject truth and good (better of two choices). Conversely whatever the intellect presents to the will as bad (worse of two choices), the will must reject.

One might reasonably ask then, how is sin possible, since we understand sin to be a willful breach of goodness? It works like this. Before we can discuss sin, we must understand its derivation. In early Old Testament times, the Jews considered whatever activity they did that was associated with problems in their lives to be sin. Later on, Moses, in an attempt to control his flock, gave the Israelites the Ten Commandments with an admonition that they were God's laws. Any breech was considered sinful. Of course, these commandments corresponded to their legal system. In other words, their societal laws were considered as moral (God's) laws. As time went on, that set of laws was extended to govern almost every minute instance of Jewish existence. When Christianity came into being and the Catholic Church was established, the list of sins included not only the Ten Commandments but also the Laws of the Church. So, in that framework, we begin to understand how sin was interpreted and how resultant remedies (punishments) were meted out. The Israelites punishment was in the form of pestilence, famine, enslavement by neighboring pagan kings etc. Christian punishment came with fire and brimstone in either purgatory or hell. My belief is that all those commandments are man-made and designed to impart guilt with resultant punishment of one kind or another. So, in that framework, with proper indoctrination (brainwashing), it is easy to see how the currant concepts of sin were developed and accepted, at least by many. In the case of the Jews, they were constantly bargaining with God in order to attempt solvency in their lives. In the case of Catholic Christianity, the bargaining continues through unrelenting petition from many sources (Virgin Mary, all the saints, friends, communities, paid priest's stipends, indulgences etc., etc.), but most if not all mediated through the Church; Jesus gave The Keys Of The Kingdom to Peter, the first Pope. It is easy to see then that the so-called commandments are set in direct opposition to any and all elements of our nature, Selfishness. With those principals in mind, it is unmistakable that literally every moment of our existence could be defined as sinful.

I have often wondered how the Israelites, knowing that their plight was caused by sin in the first place, rationalized their purchase of food from the pagan Pharos. It seems to me that, rather than accept their punishment dutifully, they chose to sin worse by circumventing God a second time. Of course, as the story goes, they did, in fact, incur a greater punishment, enslavement at the hands of the Pharos. Moses, himself was a murderer, but never-mind that; he became the self-proclaimed leader of the Jewish clan. So it is obvious that the most sinful can and do rise to the highest levels of command: I almost have to snicker thinking about some of the world leaders throughout history. In any event, sin is a matter of personal interpretation which is based primarily on two principles, namely indoctrination and perceived need. If we have accepted our indoctrination completely, it is likely that we will be in the state of some sort of sin constantly. That is because our needs outweigh, at least momentarily, our fear of reprisal. If, on the other hand, we reject our indoctrination, or if our indoctrination has been scant or absent, we would be free from sin and guilt much more of the time. This touches on the theme of conscience which I maintain is a contrived device aimed solely at external control by some man-made authority. In my opinion, there is only one sin (evil) in the universe and that is the universal evil of SELFISHNESS. As explained elsewhere, that condition was instilled into every creature and object in His universe by Almighty God Himself. The purpose of prayer is to acknowledge to God our selfishness and to thank Him for giving us value by accepting (loving) us through the death of His Son, Jesus. Jesus asked us to emulate Him by taking up our cross of accepting the annoyances of our fellow man (loving our neighbor) as He did. I believe that is the cross we have to bear; His yoke about which Jesus speaks of as being easy.

I accept the two commandments that Jesus gave us as complete (love your God and love your neighbor) that is more of a task than any of us can handle. The rituals of the church, their unrelenting concern about what we eat and when, absolute control of our sexuality, and the degrading of women in my opinion are all misguided and seemingly are designed to exercise total control over our lives. The constant and unrelenting accumulation of wealth by the church under the guise of making God happy is shameful. The un-abashed hypocrisy of, constantly, pleading for God to do something for the poor, the homeless and the starving, all the while plotting to spend millions for unneeded buildings and equipment is indeed shameful.

Over the years the church had demonized all the basic instincts that God created in man. Man is no different from any other animal in many respects. All animals have a basic drive for survival. That includes food and water, reproduction and shelter. I don't believe God cares how we go about it or even if we do. He equipped us with the tools and an intellect to use them and the rest is up to us.

From the earliest days women have been treated as second class citizens; they were basically a man's property and if another man had sex with her, she would be stoned to death, but he would basically go free (maybe a scourging, but seldom stoning to death). Jesus on the other hand is depicted as showing equal acceptance of men and women. Jesus is willing to incriminate no woman (Mary Magdalene story and the woman at the well are examples). In some cultures, married women are not allowed to show their faces; what kind of terrorism is that? Someone apparently writing in the name of the apostle Paul stated flatly that women should keep quiet, stay covered and stay pregnant; some wonderful existence eh?

The Catholic Church has steadfastly disallowed the consecration of women priests under the pretense that Jesus only chose men for HIS ministry. It is understandable that women were not chosen then for a variety of reasons, but, as best I can determine, the most compelling reason was that women were not considered to be worthy. That is born out in the last statement of Peter in the Coptic Gospel of Thomas; "let Mary leave us because women are not worthy", and Jesus reply, "I, Myself, will make her male so she will become worthy like you males", paraphrased. In my opinion, that is very prejudicial and extremely unjust. I have never observed any hesitancy by any priest or bishop to ask women to do things for them, but that's as far as it goes. Oh the Church, in an act of complete condescension, has allowed women to read the scriptures, and to give communion, but I suspect that was to prevent complete rebellion (give the dog a crumb). My research indicates that it was in the year of 1983 before a female was allowed to enter a Catholic Church Sanctuary. WHAT KIND OF DISCRIMINATION, AND SEXISM IS THAT??

CHAPTER 6

A Prescription for Success

IF THE CHURCHES AND GREAT religions truly wanted to save the world, eliminate hunger, and suppress disease, they would take bold and decisive steps as follows:

1. They would sell everything they own and distribute the proceeds in poor nations, developing business, creating jobs, building schools and medical clinics, and generally be God loving and people loving in their approach; and
2. They would create a singular TV ministry that would explain, on a continual basis, the simple truths about God; the Trinity, the universality of truth, the omnipresence of God, the perfection and goodness of God and, above all, the necessity of accepting Gods Will.

With that understanding, people could feel free to accept and understand God for what He is. People could be at peace, and the terrible, terrifying, persecuting blanket of guilt could finally be pulled off mankind. At last he could feel free to love and respect his God and his fellow man as he should.

DOES ANYONE HEAR MY CRY? DOES ANYONE CARE?

CHAPTER 7
The Bible

§

IN PRIOR DISCUSSION OF THE Old Testament, I have pointed out obvious discrepancies and unrealistic statements. More importantly, I have noted the consistent depiction of God as changeable (He likes you one day and will even kill for you, and hates you the next day to the point of letting you be tormented or even killed.) God was believed to have chosen a singular people, the Jews, as His very own, to the exclusion of all others. God is described as being vengeful, wrathful, hostile, just, merciful and generous. I have also pointed out that those precepts are incompatible with my concept of God as Perfect in all respects, and neither changing nor changeable. Nevertheless, that is the ideology promulgated in the Old Testament. The Jews believed that their vengeful God must be appeased with animal sacrifice. One Old Testament story depicts Abraham as ready and willing to kill his own son as a sacrificial appeasement of God. Of course, in modern times, that irrational and illegal activity would be met with harsh legal justice. In addition, the Jews found it necessary and desirable to have a law regulating literally every minute aspect of their daily lives; those laws were, of course, "God-given". While I have no problem understanding and accepting their attitudes at the time, I take extreme issue with the modern Christian Church perpetuating a sacrificial offering as appeasement. That attempt at legalistic control of our everyday lives is outrageous.

It should be noted that as far as I can determine the oldest known copy of New Testament in existence was made some 200 years after Jesus' death.

One can only imagine the many changes (some deliberate and others accidental) that would have occurred during the laborious task of making just one copy. There were no printing presses, and, as far as I can determine, there were very few, if any, truly literate people available to make such copies. Since there was need for a great many copies, it is unthinkable that even a single copy could be made without major mistakes. Moreover, some of those copies were translations from one language into another. Writing in some of those languages was done, not by separation of individual words and sentences, but by continuous letters of their alphabet with no punctuation (mfwuhfkrnhstyanfidjnm). One can only imagine how the original wording and meaning could and would have become altered.

Needless to say, it is unlikely that the intent of the original author was preserved. Biblical scholars have shown us that the errors and changes are many to say the least. The ultimate truth is that we simply do not know what Jesus said or did, THE ONLY REFERENCES WE HAVE ARE THE BIASED WRITINGS AND REWRITINGS OF DOCUMENTS LONG SINCE EXTINCT.

We can surmise, rightly so, that, in the early church, there was no uniform agreement about who Jesus was, nor was there any agreement about what he taught and did. That fact is evident from the numerous warring Christian factions that were in existence when Constantine became emperor of the Roman Empire. When Constantine convened the first council of Nicaea, it seems his intention was to achieve a uniform church doctrine which he enforced as a state religion to the point of exile or execution for any nonconformist. After much haggling, a majority won-out temporarily and the so called heretics were put down, at least temporarily. Emotions and belief ran high and eventually Constantine was baptized into a heretical sect (Arianism) before his death. It is highly likely that each of those separate sects were using, as basis for their beliefs, writings which had been altered from those writings being used by another sect. Some of those alterations may have been deliberate to conform to individual sect interpretations and others may have been accidental. Regardless of the cause, the net result was a conglomerate of non-uniform writings about a very complex subject. Constantine reasoned that his rule would be much easier if there were uniformity of doctrine. What eventuated was what the most influential and powerful selected to be the true scripture, but not, necessarily, what was the true scripture. Given the circumstances, I don't see how it could have been otherwise.

I am not suggesting that those *in charge* were not well meaning, holy men, but human nature being what it is, I can't conceive of such a plan not being at least somewhat self-serving. All we need do is peruse church history and observe the atrocities committed by the Church to understand the failings of *holy men*. To lend unquestioned authority to the writings, church fathers proclaimed each and every word to be inerrant. I might interject here that I don't understand how God could have gotten so mixed up. I maintain that if the bible were truly the *inspired* word of God, there would be no contradictions or discrepancies.

It is clear to me that the early writers did not consider Jesus to be God or at least not equal to the Father. Paul, the earliest writer, was grossly misinformed about Jesus' second coming; another indication of his information sources as being those whom he persecuted. In Mark and Matthew's gospel, Jesus is described as saying that the Father knows things which He does not. In John's gospel, Jesus disclaims equality with the Father saying "for the Father is greater than I". Matthew's feeble attempt at showing Jesus' lineage from David in order to fulfill a prophecy is scandalous. Joseph, Jesus' step-father descended from David but not Mary, His mother. It is possible that Matthew or someone altering Matthew's writing thought this attempt to *marry* the Old Testament prophecy with New Testament fact would be more compelling and most people, being illiterate, wouldn't know the difference. I am aware that some biblical scholars attempt to show Mary's lineage as coming though David, but, seemingly, most are not in accord. In Matthew's gospel, Joseph flees to Egypt with Jesus and Mary to escape Herod's wrath. However, in Luke, they return home to Nazareth almost immediately after Jesus' circumcision. God really stays confused when telling stories of biblical proportion, or so it seems. The Christian church continues to proclaim the idea of an inerrant bible. It seems that they, like Matthew belittle and scorn us by assuming we are too ignorant and stupid to know the difference. I may, in fact, be stupid and ignorant but I think I recognize a fairy tale when I hear one.

It is obvious that the New Testament writers were intent on making Old Testament prophesies come true because of the repeated statements that such and such happened to fulfill the scriptures.

My opinion: at best, the New Testament is composed of documents written by mere mortals who had a direct bias or prejudice based on their Jewish culture and their interpretation of the events surrounding Jesus or stories about Jesus. Their direct attempt to meld Jesus' presence with their predetermined concepts of a heavenly kingdom on earth with them as *the beneficiaries* is evident. That seems to be the main point of contention in their early church. What Jesus really did and said, what His birth, childhood, ministry, crucifixion, resurrection, and ascension were really like, we probably will never know in this life. It seems unquestionable that we have no reliable source of truth.

As I have said before, the only way the Last Supper makes sense (assuming of course that it really took place), is for Jesus to have recognized that His soul mirrored that of God. This I believe as a matter of faith supported by both philosophical and scientific logic. This is the ONLY faith I have.

CHAPTER 8

The Unholy Triumvirate

§

FOR YEARS I HAVE NOTICED that certain scripture readings appearing in the Sunday liturgy were never addressed in the homily. In the beginning I ignored that fact thinking that maybe the priest had another point to discuss. As the years went by, it became so noticeable, that I began to mentally question why that might be. The reason eventually became clear; those readings were in direct opposition to Catholic Church teaching. In light of that recognition, I have given those scripture readings the general title of *unholy triumvirate* because recognition of their validity would *invalidate* Church teaching and, more importantly, would negate the need for the Church's existence. Those three scripture segments are as follows:

1. Paul's repeated assertion that salvation is wrought solely through *Faith in Jesus:*
   A few examples are as follows:
   a. "for we hold that man is justified by faith apart from observance of the law" (Romans 3: 28),
   b. "Nevertheless, knowing that man is not justified by legal observance but by faith in Jesus Christ, we too have believed in him in order to be justified by faith in Christ, not by observance of the law." (Galatians 2: 16)
   c. "In Christ Jesus neither circumcision nor the lack of it account for anything: only faith, which expresses itself through love". (Galatians 5: 6)

d. "It is in Christ and through his blood that we have been redeemed and our sins forgiven, so immeasurably generous is God's favor for us." (Ephesians 1: 7-8)
e. "I repeat, it is owing to His favor that salvation is yours through faith. This is not your own doing, it is God's gift; neither is it a reward for anything you have accomplished, so let no one pride himself on it". (Ephesians 2: 8-9)
f. "Even when you were dead in sin and your flesh was uncircumcised, God gave you new life in company with Christ. He pardoned all our sins". (Colossians 2: 13
g. Those assertions by Paul are in complete opposition to Church teaching which states emphatically that we must *work* our way into heaven. This working is done in the first instance by observing not only the Ten Commandments but, just as importantly, the Laws of the Church. It entails every sort of contrived devotion to the Blessed Mother of Jesus, as well as, to specific Saints (those whom the Church have pronounced without doubt to be in heaven). We are encouraged to beg God, ourselves, to do us no eternal harm, but we are advised that the Virgin Mary and the saints have much more *bargaining power than we*.
h. However, the most powerful source of supplication comes to us through the institution of the Church which, through the hands of the Pope, holds the *keys to the kingdom of God.*

   Paul considered Jesus' death to be complete exoneration of all our evil; all we had to do was *accept* and believe. The Church, on the other hand, does not accept Jesus' death as complete for our salvation (please note *the implication* that not even God is powerful enough to forgive us completely); we must suffer in *purgatory* to burn away the *stain* of sin before admission to heaven is possible.
i. Now, of course, there are certain prayers that we may say to lessen our *time* in torment. Those prayers carry an

indulgence of varying length (a period of lessened sentence). Those indulgence bearing prayer and their specific sentence reducing time were designed by the church. There was once a time in Church history when those who could afford it, *rich people*, could buy indulgences. That, of course, served two very important functions; it enabled the desperate rich ("it is easier for a camel to pass through a needle's eye than for a rich man to enter the kingdom of God") to have some glimmer of hope. More importantly, it replenished the Vatican coffers which had been depleted by previous, irresponsible squandering popes.

2. As stated in Mark 12: 29-31, Jesus gave us two commandments by which to live; "Hear, oh Israel! The Lord our God is Lord alone! Therefore you shall love the Lord our God with all your heart, with all your soul, with all your mind, and with all your strength. This is the second, you shall love your neighbor as yourself." Those two commandments completely negate the need for an organizational structure comprised of thousands of administrators officiating from thousands of monstrous edifices costing billions, maybe even trillions, of dollars to erect and maintain. Those simple *truths could be promulgated* in communities by local leaders as a repeated reminder of our simple relationship and obligation to God and our neighbor. There is not the slightest implication in those two directives for a need of the *saving grace of the sacraments, novenas, first Fridays, tridua, and the like*; no need for *the mass with the recreation of Jesus*. That, of course, obviates the need for priests with special powers to perform those duties on our behalf. In short, *no need nor justification for* an organizational religion of any sort.

3. In 1 John 3: 2 we see John declare; "Dearly beloved, we are Gods children now; what we shall later be has not yet come to light. We know that when it comes to light we shall be like Him for we shall see Him as he is". The implications of this statement are so far-reaching. The Church's doctrine regarding heaven maintains that

God is *sitting* on a throne and Jesus is *sitting* at His right hand. It doesn't say where the Holy Ghost is (I suppose He doesn't count very much). It goes without saying that if we could see God as He truly is and we are like Him, then we *are Him. We all are sitting on a throne with Jesus at our right hand.* (Poor Holy Ghost; I bet He feels *left out.*) All of this completely negates the Church's dogma that heaven is a place where we will be reunited with our body and with our family and friends in a humanistic sort of perfect happiness; however, some will be in a higher place (front row seat) than others, and I suppose with that comes a greater degree of happiness. Sounds selfish to me. John's understanding transcends anything human and goes straight to the Ultimate; we will be God because we are of Him always.

4. It is easy to see then why the aforementioned set of readings are never, ever addressed in homilies. What can a priest, bishop, or pope say about them that wouldn't discredit either the church or the Bible? Nothing. So nothing is ever said. Oh, the Church, in an attempt to show they have nothing to hide, sticks those scripture readings right out in front of our noses. But they do hide behind a veil of silence leaving us to quandary over their meaning. They are deliberately silent and we are *silenced* because we are not allowed to ask questions. Consequently, we are *left in the dark*.

CHAPTER 9
Evil in the Universe

§

IF WE DESCRIBE EVIL AS *THAT CONDITION OF SELFISHNESS*, then we can say with relative certainty that the entire universe and all its gross components are intrinsically evil. That is easily demonstrated in the plant and animal kingdoms, and even in the inanimate world, some instances more obvious than others. In the human race, there exists a common and consistent attitude of *me first*. Each human wants *his space* and generally always at the expense of other's space. While we try in some degree or another to be *sharing* with others, there probably never exists a perfect attitude in that regard. Likewise, in the remainder of the animal kingdom, we note the common trait of *survival of the fittest*, which is just another way of saying *I am bigger and stronger or smarter than you and therefore I get more space*. In the vegetable world, we see that *attitude* born out in many individual ways, but usually in similar fashion. For instance, large trees shade smaller undergrowths, depriving them of vital sunlight, water and nutrients. Larger, more aggressive, weeds overpower less aggressive grasses and vegetables, choking them out of healthy existence. More aggressive grasses such as Bermuda grass overpower less aggressive such as bent grass and force them into a debilitated state and finally extinction. And so it goes on and on in animal and vegetable world. In the inanimate world, we see similar activity. Each rock or grain of sand bears down upon its neighbors, hollowing out a space for itself at its neighbor's expense. The weather elements, *wind, rain, sunlight, floodwaters, lightening etc.*, all are displacing and altering both animate and inanimate existences so as to *appease their appetites*. Asteroids and comets are continually bombarding planets and other stellar bodies, so to speak, making room for themselves. On a much larger scale, galaxies are devouring other entire galaxies in the grandest show of bullying yet.

So, recognizing this universal condition of evil, one might reasonably ask why and how, if God made this universe to be perfect and to function perfectly in every respect, can it be universally evil? I accept that there may be two possible reasons. One would be that evil is a man-made concept and of no concern to God. This, indeed, would be a simplistic explanation, but does not address or explain Jesus and his heroic death for our salvation. The second explanation has to do with LOVE, GOD'S PERFECT LOVE.

If we accept that God is perfect in all things, then we admit to His Perfect Love. One might ask, what is love? In the abstract, love is only a concept; a concept that encompasses a giver and a receiver. Without a recipient love does not exist in reality, only in concept. Perfect Love means in concept *total acceptance without conditions*. If God is to have Perfect Love, He must have a worthy recipient. What more *worthy recipient* could God have than an entire universe or universes of evil which He, Himself, created?

I accept that there were no Adam and Eve, as such, who ate of the forbidden fruit causing evil in the world; it was God Himself. He planned that from all eternity as a means of being *PERFECT LOVE* and, in so doing, he has guaranteed our eternal salvation. No matter how much we turn against God; no matter what horrendous things we do, His perfect Love never ceases. Our job, our cross, our yoke is to shrink our own space so others may have their space; Jesus said "love your neighbor as yourself".

One might reasonably argue or ask how it is possible for God to be Perfect Love from all eternity, when the exhibition of that Love only occurred 2000 years ago. The answer lies in the fact that eternity has no time, *no beginning nor end*. God has always been Perfect Love in His conceptualization (intention); its' demonstration in the material, temporal world for us to see is what occurred 2000years ago. It goes without saying then, that God always conceptualized (intended) the *need* for a suitable vehicle to *allow* His being Perfect Love. That explains the concept of a *need* for an evil universe of total selfishness.

CHAPTER 10

Evolution of evil

§

IT SEEMS APPARENT THAT EARLIEST Homo sapiens had little, if any, concept of *loving thy neighbor as thyself.* That is borne out by the numerous archeological accounts of skeletal remains demonstrating evidence of brute trauma. Some of those certainly could have resulted from animal attacks and others from falls, rockslides, etc.; however many undoubtedly were from direct personal confrontation. This certainly is reasonable since man evolved from a system of *survival of the fittest*, and would have had little, if any, natural inclination to be charitable and loving as a first effort. In all likelihood, the maternal instinct to protect her baby, possibly even from other male aggressors, would have fueled the fire of self-preservation, thereby setting up a natural state of general hostility to others. Even the *ice man* was killed by an assailant who chased him up a mountain 4000 years, or so, ago. I accept that it is reasonable to assume that eventually common sense prevailed and small groups began to see the benefits of banding together for their common good of cooperative hunting and defending against wild animals as well as other human groups.

However, it is most certain that within those individual groups, there were those who dominated the others. Eventually, those groups grew and banded together for the common good into larger tribes and, ultimately, states and nations. And so we see from the earliest recorded history, the story is basically the same; we have kings and peasants, we have master and slave, we have the haves and the have-nots. In essence, our society is little different from any animal society. While it is true, that the scriptures depict many examples of seemingly genuine love of neighbor, the general rule is just the opposite; someone or some tribe or some nation warring with another incessantly. In the Old Testament, many of those battles with both victory and defeat are ascribed to the direct influence of God.

It is very apparent, that by the time Jesus appeared on the scene, there was little, if any, genuine neighborly love in existence. The biblical as well as secular records indicate conclusively that the attitude among people in general was simply *me first, dog eat dog, the biggest wins* just like in the wild animal kingdom. However, mankind introduced another element into the picture; one seldom seen outside the human race, except possibly in foxes and weasels, and that condition we call cunning and greed.

History and everyday observation will show us that Jesus' command, to "love your neighbor as yourself", has been totally ignored. Those who have usurped the authority and the power as protectors and advisors on such matters, the Church, have totally ignored that command. Instead, they have busied themselves with declaring thousands of rules and regulations regarding every minute aspect of human life, ostensibly, to maintain control and power and wealth for the Church and themselves. Preaching the simple truth, the Gospel, *the Good News that Jesus suffered and died for our salvation*, and explaining Jesus command would not add to the power base. People would soon realize that all the rules the church exercises over them are meaningless. The simple truth demands no massive cathedrals and edifices of all sorts; Jesus, while he preached at times in the synagogues, is most often depicted preaching and teaching in a simple natural setting. I don't know of any place in scripture where Jesus suggest that God, His Father, would be the least bit impressed with any massive, expensively adorned building; neither am I aware of His proclaiming, that a tirade of singing and musical instrument playing are beneficial at all. To the contrary, I suspect that God would look with great disdain on such activity as being naive, stupid, and, more importantly, shamefully wasteful. As a matter of acceptance, I don't think God cares one way or the other. Garry Wills, in his studious book, "What Paul Meant", concludes that religion took over the legacy of both Jesus and Paul; they both despised religion. They said that the love of God was a personal matter; they issued two dictums, love of God and love of neighbor. In spite of our sinful, egotistical, hostile, aggressive, proud and controlling ways, God loves (accepts) us just the same.

So here we are, a society of rational people who have never, never, ever, been directed on the proper course by their assumed leaders. To do so would mean the end of organized religion as we know it. There would be no bible thumping preachers making lavish livings *interpreting* every single word of the bible to prove a power point only to have the next bible thumper making just as extravagant a living *proving* a diametrically opposed point with the same passage. There would be no preachers trying to explain away obvious contradictions in the bible, insulting the common sense of all.

But no, nothing will change; the charade will go on; people will be demonized from every pulpit in the world; they will drag their guilt ridden persona through this hell hole until, finally, they find peace in Jesus at death. Every God-given instinct that we have has been condemned, and demonized to the extreme, ostensibly for total exercise of power and control. The charade is played out very clearly, in the so called stewardship program. One's involvement is encouraged as a means of making him/her feel important in this ruse; likewise our talents are extolled and wooed almost always for free (you're working for God); but more importantly, they want your money. They rile and rant from the pulpit about the poor and the homeless and the generally depraved, but in my lifetime, I have not witnessed any genuine, concerted effort by organized religion to attend to the needs of the poor and homeless. In that regard, I recently had a young priest point out that in Luke's gospel, Jesus is quoted as saying that the poor, the hungry and depraved are, in fact blessed. If that be the case, then I see the church as being extremely hypocritical in continually pointing out these people and that we should be helping them. The truth seems to me to be that if these people are blessed, we certainly should not interfere with God's work; rather we should work at being more like them. Even Mother Theresa worked to help the needy. I rather suspect Luke had a different angle; even though Luke was Greek, he seemed to have the same bias as the other early biblical writers who were Jews, and who had obviously similar bias, as their writings demonstrate. I accept that, if Jesus said anything, it would be Matthew's version, "Blessed are the poor in spirit"; a completely different concept. It is possible for one to be the richest person on earth and still be poor in spirit. What I have observed, however, is a continuing campaign to build the organized religion empire. We are asked, even demanded, to contribute to those campaigns under the guise of giving to God which pleases Him. I don't accept that line of reasoning at all; God can neither be pleased nor displeased. The pleasure comes to those who are instigating such projects, in the belief that they are increasing their stature with God, *buying their way into heaven*. Is that not tantamount to buying and selling indulgences?

Consider this; if each person could *love his neighbor as himself*, which he cannot, there would be no strife in the world. There would be total peace and contentment. There would be no hostility, no wars, no fights and no uneasiness; there would be nothing but pure love, peace and serenity. I accept that Jesus' command to *love your neighbor as yourself* is the cross Jesus speaks of when he says, "take up your cross and follow me". That is what Jesus did; he loved each of us without reservation or condition; his command to us, our cross, is to do likewise. Regrettably, the churches have ignored Jesus command; SHAME, SHAME, SHAME ON THEM.

CHAPTER 11

What About Selfishness?

§

SELFISHNESS MAY BE DEFINED AS any activity, idea, or consideration directed at self. As explained before, selfishness is necessary for our existence. As a society, we accept a moderate degree of selfishness as desirable and useful. On the other hand, we consider an extreme degree of selfishness to be offensive and undesirable. Often times, we may consider it to be sinful, illegal or both. How then can those two extremely opposite degrees of selfishness be reconciled as one?

Jesus gave us guide-lines, *love our neighbor as ourselves.* Some think of this suggestion as a *commandment.* I rather think Jesus was suggesting that dictum as a means to joy and happiness; *the more we care, share and give, the happier we will be.*

Why then do some people seem to be more selfish than others? The answer lies in individual personality development. Attitudes learned by being led down the wrong path cause each of us to be innately selfish to a degree different from anyone else. That is possible because each of our life's experiences are different. Therefore, it is extremely important that each of us understand that fact, and, thereby, make allowances for each other's differences. I accept Jesus' saying *my yoke is easy* was His way of expressing His unconditional acceptance of us all. He suggests that we make our yoke easier by Imitating Him. Even though we will never succeed completely as He did, our continual attempt will enrich our lives with happiness, peace and joy. The obvious implication here, then, is that all our emphasis should be directed at proper training and discipline in the concept of love (acceptance) from infancy on.

The Church (s), by totally ignoring Jesus' command are the prime *culprit* in unwittingly promoting *extreme* selfishness. Their emphasis is on rituals and rules all the while demeaning every God-given instinct of human nature. That doctrinal process only frustrates people and creates inner feelings of guilt, anger and anxiety, all of which are acted out in their daily lives. The obvious visible result is a greater degree of selfishness exhibited by parents, teachers and associates, all the while being observed and learned by children. This sequence sets up an unrelenting journey down the wrong path. For many this path leads to extreme breeches of societal rules such as murder, rape, theft, terrorism etc.

It is the Churches' responsibility to teach and promote concepts of love (acceptance). Sadly, sadly, their *only* emphasis seems to be on growing the *Empire of money, control and power.*

Our constitution, rightly so, defines a concept of separation of Church and state. IN spite of that, if all churches, Christian, Muslim, Jew, and others alike, promoted, as a first effort, the concept of loving neighbor as self, soon enough, it would become an innate principle in the attitudes of our public school teachers. That principle would become the main-thread of all teaching, and, as such, would not and could not be considered as *religious* teaching. It should and, rightly so, would be considered the prime *social and psychological* principle of life and living.

I firmly accept that all the strife and turmoil exhibited in the world throughout history is due to a complete lack of understanding and application of Jesus' principle. Love of neighbor (acceptance) is mandatory for peace and happiness. WHERE ARE THE CHURCHES?

CHAPTER 12

God In the Universe

§

I READ, WITH GREAT ADMIRATION, Dr. Bart Ehrman's book, *God's Problem*. His thoroughness in addressing the subject of suffering as depicted in the bible combined with his complete knowledge of the bible are, simply put, astonishing. However, accompanying my feelings of great exhilaration, and admiration of his brilliance, is a deep sense of sadness and pity for him as a human being and brother. Without a doubt, he seems to have lost his belief in God based on his inability to understand how a good God could allow such unbelievable misery and suffering in the world. At the same time, he can find no suitable answer in the bible, the one source that organized fundamentalist religion has always claimed to contain all the answers. His complete understanding of the bible has exposed its' innumerable discrepancies, contradictions, and misrepresentations. In spite of recognizing the untrustworthiness of the bible, he has given it a *fair trial* at answering the imponderable questions with which we are confronted. He is able to find *no* consistent or suitable solutions. As a result, he has concluded that there is no suitable explanation of Gods existence nor, more importantly, His MO (mode of operation). As a result, he has reluctantly given up on God. That is, indeed, a sad state of affairs as he freely admits.

I, like Dr.Ehrman, once enjoyed the warm, consoling, comforting, reliant relationship associated with my religion. Also, like him, I soon began to notice gross discrepancies between what I was taught to believe and what I was able to observe. Those discrepancies, in turn, led to my *journey of understanding*, as described in my previous discussion. My religious developmental background prompted a different type of *understanding of God* rather than a refusal to accept His existence. Dr. Ehrman, on the other hand, simply threw up his hands, so to speak, and said, "I quit- I can't believe". His reaction becomes understandable when one considers the fundamentalist culture in which he was raised and educated. Fundamentalism gives quarter to no outside influence regarding God, morality and religion other than the bible. In my instance that was not the case.

    I was taught that Catholic doctrine emanated not only from the bible, but also from tradition. In fact, when I was a child, Catholics were advised not to read the bible; we were not intelligent enough to make proper interpretations. It was only in later years, after fundamentalist televangelism became so popular and financially successful by preaching the bible, that, seemingly, the Catholic Church decided it was desirable and necessary to begin emphasizing the bible and its formal study. In past times, the scriptures were read at mass, just as now. However, the homilies (sermons) seldom were about anything concerning the biblical readings; rather, they, more often than not, were ranting's about observing church law; mostly concerning artificial birth control, tithing, fasting and abstinence from eating meat on prescribed days, mixed marriage (marrying a non-Catholic), and last but not least mandatory attendance at mass on every Sunday and Holy Day Of Obligation (days the church established in honor of some saint or saints; there even was a Holy Day [January I] each year in honor of Jesus' circumcision. The bible definitely was not the main focus of attention. Nowadays, the Bible (church missal from which the scriptures are read), is held high and paraded by the priest from altar to pulpit while glorifying intonations are made. I have often wondered why this sudden emphasis on the bible. My suspicion is that Catholic authorities have taken note of the attraction to potential converts created by the televangelists.

    So, in Dr. Ehrman's case, having little essential exposure to religion other than biblical fundamentalism, when that failed him, all was lost; there was no other source or recourse; God simply didn't exist or couldn't be trusted.

In my case realizing that my religious culture probably emanated as much from tradition (rules, regulations and understandings based on hearsay) as from the bible, I felt not only free but obligated to try, as best I could, to discover the truth. In that sense I consider myself a Prophet every bit as much as the prophets of the Old Testament. God gave me an intellect just as he did them; they saw it as necessary to explore and explain problems and situations then; I feel the same necessity now. I, in all humility, recognize that I, in fact, may not be right, but I definitely am not in doubt. I am right until someone proves me wrong. At the very least, I have developed a scheme of God, the universe and their interrelation that is both scientifically and philosophically sound. That is more than anyone else I am aware of has done.

I have redefined God and His workings. The Biblical God was changeable; loving and helpful one minute, and vengeful and hateful the next. My God is Perfect and Unchangeable in all respects. Recognizing that fact brings me easily and comfortably into God's realm; all I need do is Accept His Will, *whatever comes my way* as best I can, and, at the same time, Love My Neighbor As Myself, as best I can; *an insurmountable task*. I hope and pray that Dr. Bart Ehrman can see this light and come to similar acceptance. He truly is a beautiful, loving, caring, brilliant man. His EMPTINESS saddens me immeasurably; he is suffering unnecessarily. I dread thinking of all the others who suffer because of the similar misguidance of organized religion.

CHAPTER 13

Universality of God

※

THERE IS AN ENTIRE SEGMENT of Christianity which seems to profess the idea that God is an entity separate and apart from all the elements of nature, including humanity. Their ideology controls God by *pigeon holing* Him and putting Him in a separate place apart from all other existences. They attempt to humanize God by relegating Him to a certain location both in heaven and on earth. Also, they reduce God to the belittled state of being subject to influence and manipulation. This is borne out in the Old Testament by the act of keeping God under *lock and key*', so to speak, in the Arc of the Covenant. Modern Catholicism and its near mimickers have interpreted the Last Supper of Jesus Christ to be a mandate to recreate Him out of bread and wine and distribute that newly created Body and Blood of Jesus to the faithful. The left overs, *Jesus parceled*, is stored in a gold tabernacle where no one can see, *modern day Arc of the Covenant*. On special reverence occasions, Jesus body is displayed in a gold monstrance for the faithful to worship. This ideology and activity certifies the belief of the hierarchy that they are in control of God's whereabouts. They have conveniently interpreted Jesus' words at the Last Supper to mean exactly that. That, of course, is completely self-serving, as it gives them total control not only of all people but of God Himself.

My opinion, based on science, the Coptic Gospel of Thomas, (*The Secret Sayings Of Jesus Christ*) and common sense philosophy, is just the opposite. I accept that God's perfect intellect and power are manifested in the absolute perfection, in both form and function, of each and every atomic and subatomic particle of matter. I accept that, with His Perfect Intellect, God perceived the change of His power into matter particles and He empowered them with His Holy Spirit (Will) to be perfect in form and function until such time as He determines otherwise. Without reservation, I accept that Jesus' saying "this is My body and this is My blood", (paraphrased), at His last supper was His way of telling the apostles one final time that He is in all things and all things are in Him. That explains why the writer of John's gospel didn't mention the Last Supper as such. Although John likely had no earthly idea how that could be, he recognized what Jesus was saying, and therefore set about showing Jesus' universal Divinity. Even though John probably did not write his gospel, himself, it is without doubt that his followers were well acquainted with his teachings. Unquestionably, had Jesus meant the Eucharistic Feast (the recreation of Jesus from bread and wine) to be the centerpiece of His fledgling church, John not only would have told the story in full account, but would have emphasized it dramatically. Rather, I accept that John understood perfectly what Jesus was saying. I might interject, however, that John was not able to stay completely convinced of Jesus' equality with the Father, because he quotes Jesus as saying "for the Father is greater than I". To me this indicates some confusion on John's part about the absolute degree of Jesus' divinity.

The Coptic Gospel of Thomas, which was rejected by the first council of Nicaea as a biblical canon, quotes Jesus' saying over and over the same thing in different words, namely, "I am in all things and all things are in Me" (paraphrased). The reason for the rejection is obvious. That concept of the universality of Jesus (God) negated the council members desire of keeping God separate and controlled by them; no longer could they assume a stance of recreating and storing God; they would lose all regimental power over God and His people. Since Constantine The Great was giving them free reign over the destiny of all humanity, they were not about to give up that control.

It is scientific fact that light travels at a rate of roughly 186,000 miles per second. It is also a scientific fact that light which has been travelling

13.7 billion years is just now reaching our earth. Those facts allude to the size of God's universe; a size and dimension that no human mind can comprehend. It follows then, that our God, who made and sustains this entire universe and, undoubtedly more, is larger, more powerful, and more perfect than any mere mortal can imagine. How is it then that we modern men are still mired in a morass of ancient mythological and superstitious thinking? The answer seems clear to me. The church has created an empire of both property and control. If they admitted to that truth, organized religion would instantly be nullified and obsolete. All the power and control over people's minds and money would be lost. The need for clergy would instantly be abolished. The superstitious charade would cease and people would be free to recognize their God in all things; more importantly, they would be free to accept God's Will (which is each and every occurrence), rather than attempting to "do" God's Will which is unknowable. We would be free then to concentrate on the first half of The Lord's Prayer and the commands that I believe Jesus gave us to love God with our all and to love our neighbor as ourselves. It is impossible to execute the first command without executing the second and visa-versa. Suffice it to say, no mere mortal human will ever succeed. Therein lies the beauty and thrill of Jesus' ultimate sacrifice and Perfect Love!

CHAPTER 14

The Holy Spirit

WHO OR WHAT IS THE Holy Spirit? It would be impossible to make that determination from biblical descriptions. No definition is offered. It is described as the paraclete (one who walks beside) in one place. In another It is simply conferred by Jesus; "receive ye the holy spirit………". In Luke's Acts of the Apostles, the Holy Spirit is described as tongues of fire descending upon the apostles accompanied by strong winds and thunderous roars. Paul says "we are temples of the Holy Spirit".

None of the above references clearly define what or who the Holy Spirit is. Each of them leave the impression that the Holy Spirit is some ill-defined entity that serves in different capacities. One such capacity seems to impart the power of God to forgive sins. Another seems to allow for the miraculous instantaneous ability to speak multiple heretofore unknown languages. And yet another would seem to indicate a bodyguard or at least a friendly side-kick. Paul gets personal by saying the Holy Spirit resides in each of us but fails to explain where or how.

My contention is based on the principle that we and everything in existence are the direct result of the intellect (imagination) of God, mirrored by His Son, and empowered by their joint Holy Will, The Holy Spirit of God. With that understanding, we can see how Paul's allusion becomes true. The Spirit of God (Will of God) resides in us as our *existence giving principle*. Without that existence giving principle, nothing could be.

John's assertion that Jesus breathed on the apostles and said "receive the Holy Spirit…….." was a power conferring device. That is understandable because by the time John's gospel was written, transfer of power from higher to lower ministers was already common practice and the norm, the Hallmark of the early Christian church. It clearly fails though to recognize the innate presence of the Holy Spirit in any and all existences. That demonstrates, without doubt, John's lack of understanding of the Trinity, and consequently his lack of conviction of the divine equality of Jesus with the Father. At least that is the implication we garner from the bible we have now. What John really knew and thought, we have no idea. As explained previously our current versions simply cannot be trusted.

Luke's description of the Holy Spirit coming as tongues of fire with great atmospheric upheaval indicate without a doubt his miniscule, if any, appreciation of the relationship of God the Father and Son with the Holy Spirit in the Trinity. Being a zealot, his obvious intention was to impress readers with God's power but falls woefully short with wind and atmospheric saber rattling. Moreover, he tries to make us believe that the magic thus imparted could cause mere illiterates to become stupefying orators in any and all foreign languages. For the following reason, that assertion brings into question the duration of the Holy Spirit's influence on us. In studying the proposed history of the gospel authors, it is asserted that John Mark, the author of the first gospel, was a companion of Paul. However when Peter was approaching Rome, Paul loaned Mark to Peter to be his interpreter. The question immediately arises why should Peter need an interpreter? How and when did Peter lose the ability to speak and understand all languages? Is the Holy Spirit's influence temporary? If so, what is the purpose of the sacrament of Confirmation, conferring the Holy Spirit on us? Is that temporary also? We have seen clearly in Garry Wills' book, What Paul Meant, how Luke is a veritable liar and cannot be believed or trusted. Luke painted a picture which fit his miniscule imagination, or more importantly, the tiny imagination of his readers (he might be considered a romanticist).

The designation of the Holy Spirit as "the paraclete" again implies without doubt that the Holy Spirit is an entity *set aside* from our inner being. That description fails miserably to recognize the Holy Spirit as *the existence giving* principle.

The Catholic Church in its' sacrament of Confirmation asserts that the Spirit of God is under the absolute control of the Bishop, or in case of emergency, his designee. By "laying on of hands" and saying the words the power of the Holy Spirit is transferred from bishop to those being confirmed.

All of the above examples make sense when one considers the ideology which prompted them. Firstly, the Jews kept God (one person God- no Trinity God) in the Arc of The Covenant. They carried Him around on their shoulders wherever they went. Secondly, the Catholic Church keeps Jesus locked up in a gold tabernacle, and thirdly, the Catholic Church keeps the Holy Spirit under the hands of its' Bishops. Does anyone besides me see the arrogance here? We profess a God that created the entire universe with all its' unbelievable and unimaginable size, complexity and energy. Yet the Church proclaims the authority and power to dish out that God to whomever and whenever it chooses? I don't think so. Do you?

My Acceptance:

-there is God.
-He exists as Trinity.
-He is perfect and unchangeable.
-He created a % 100 evil universe so He could be Perfect Love by dying in atonement.
-We and all existences are by Him, of Him, and in Him; therefore we are Him.
-Heaven is a *state of eternal being without change*; not a place.
- If I had God's mind, I could and would gladly tell you why He chose that method. The best I can say is *He did it because He wanted to.*

All of the above observations, assertion and conclusions are based on one outstanding principle: Jesus the Christ was % 100 Homo sapiens. Like us he was purely and simply human. I accept without doubt that he was an intellectual genius who saw through the relationship between God and His universe, including mankind. He freely admitted that God knew things he did not know. However, he recognized that ultimately God is our inner being, our existence giving principal; therefore we are God.

Had he been speaking with the intellect and authority of God himself, there is little doubt that any confusion and misrepresentation of his words would have ensued. His exact words would have been *set in stone* forever with no chance for change nor misrepresentation. Jesus obviously saw *the big picture* and tried desperately to articulate that picture to his illiterate apostles. Their inability to understand coupled with their Jewish indoctrination made it impossible for Jesus to communicate a complete insight and understanding of his new teachings. As described elsewhere, there is an assertion that Judas was the only apostle to fully comprehend Jesus' teachings. The resultant mass confusion and consternation that has existed in the Christian church since Christ's death are therefore completely understandable. Moreover, they should and would have been anticipated.

The basic problem persists because of the continuing assertion of the man Jesus' divinity and the many myths regarding his birth, life, death and thereafter. Jesus the man was not divine but his inner being and life-giving principle were completely divine.

CHAPTER 15

The Holy Spirit (Will of God) Explained

If we accept that the Holy Spirit, the third person of the Blessed Trinity, represents the Living Love (Acceptance, Choice, Will) of the Father and Son in eternal and perpetual state, then we can readily see the resultant: two massive energies mirroring each other but in opposite directions. The one energy (Spirit) we call electron with a negative direction. The other energy (Spirit) we call positron with positive direction.

Given that I am in no way a particle physicist, my understanding is that if an electron and a positron collides, the result would be the total annihilation of each other accompanied by a massive release of energy. It is also my understanding that the electron represents visible matter in the universe, and that the positron represents antimatter or the, as yet, nonvisible matter in the universe. It is also my understanding that for every electron there is a corresponding positron. That is to say that for everything visible in this universe there is an invisible counterpart. One might say then that God the Father is in charge of one universe and God the Son is in charge of the other. However since there is no direction in the supernatural state of God's existence, we can comfortably say that both Father and Son are always simultaneously in charge of both universes. This might in some philosophical way explain how a given electron and presumably a given positron can and apparently do exist in more than one place at the same time. Hawking has shown that a given electron can be in something like 1×10 to the power of 50 exponential 0's at the same time. He therefore postulates that there are likely that many universes in existence.

One might reasonably ask, what keeps those universes from colliding and totally self-destructing? Philosophically, one can say with reasonable certainty, that since the Father and Son have chosen (willed) it the way it is, it is not likely to change. Rather, it will continue on in absolute perfect fashion until, and only if, They will it otherwise. Thus God has ordained (willed) those particles to be and to act perfectly as long as they exist.

What then would be God's ultimate Will? One could theorize on that point. It seems that every galaxy has a massive Black Hole in its center. In addition it seems there are many other smaller black holes wandering each galaxy devouring individual suns and planets. We also seem to know that from time to time galaxies collide and presumably their black holes coalesce. Arguably, as time goes on, the massive black hole in each galaxy's center will devour the entire galaxy. As larger black holes form, their massive gravity would pull lesser black holes into themselves until the entire visible material universe was devoured and returned to The Singularity. Similar and exact activity would be taking place in the invisible universe of the positron. Now, since Einstein's theory of gravity postulates that all matter is suspended on a fabric, it is rational to accept that when all visible matter is compressed into one black hole, the weight would be sufficient to rupture the fabric and release all that matter into a new void universe simultaneously being vacated by all the antimatter in a corresponding White Hole by its rupturing the fabric and releasing all its matter into the universe being vacated by the black hole; simultaneous "Big Bangs" from two *Singularities*, one seen, one not seen. That concept seems to explain God's ultimate power, His infinite knowledge, His unrelenting Perfection, His perpetual existence in multiple Polarities, but more importantly, His Perfect Love (His perpetual choosing (Will-Holy Spirit) of this Perfect Truth.

Presuming the foregoing hypothesis to be true in gross form, and accepting the eternal nature of God, one could draw several logical conclusions:

1. The universe, as we know it is finite and eventual total destruction is inevitable;
2. The creation of a new universe identical to previous one could be expected;

3. No information from previous universe could or would be lost; and/or
4. Those processes probably have and will continue to repeat themselves infinitely as God is Infinite.

One would be "hard pressed" to limit God's domain to what we perceive as one or two universes. More likely, our universe represents only one set of trillions of universes or other existences beyond our comprehension.

Suffice it to say, the foregoing conceptualization allows one an inkling of insight into God's perfection, power and love.

CHAPTER 16

Omni God

§

IF WE ADMIT TO THE universality of God, A Perfect Rational Being, then we must conclude that all existences are contained in God. Simply stated, there can be no existence outside God. We, as humans, are familiar with our universe only, but it is rational to assume that there may be and probably are other existences of which we have no knowledge. I say that because I accept that God's Perfect Truth must permeate any existence in order for it to be. I accept that God operates in a self- contained system. He *feeds* off Himself, but nothing basically changes because He is Perfect and unchangeable. Allow me to elucidate that very important point farther. God exists in one simple presence, ENERGY. That energy is manifested to our rationality to date in the form of sub atomic particles. These particles (energies) may have different phases at any given time, but ultimately remain the same. Therefore, there is only one substance (energy) recognizable in our universe which forms all the visible and invisible *matter* known to us. That energy, of course, is the Perfect, Unchanging *Substance* of God.

If our known universe is the only existence, then we could comfortably say that God, in totality, is contained in our universe, and our universe, in totality, is contained in God. I am not willing to concede that God's Truth and Perfection could be limited to one existence, our known universe, as vast as it is. While we, in our current human existence, may never know of other existences outside our universe, I strongly suspect that there are many others.

In any event, my ultimate point of argument is simply this. God exists in a self- contained, Perfect Truth system which is unchangeable. One might respond that change is evident everywhere, timelessly. Not so. What we see and perceive as *change* is simply the relocation and reapplication of God's particulate energy, but ultimately there is no change in the energy itself. Consider this: if we had a pile of identical bricks, we could build many different structures, but the basic building blocks are identical, unchanged and unchangeable. How then does this concept relate to our Totally Selfish Universe?

God in his infinite Perfection had a *NEED*, an object of forgiveness on which to bestow His Perfect Acceptance in order to be Perfect Love. That object is easily and clearly demonstrable in this universe of total selfishness (evil). I would suspect without ability to prove that all other existences would fit into the same category. One could retort that if God had a NEED, He was not perfect. We must understand that such a Need is part of Gods perfection which allows for Perfect Love. Of course, as stated before, the death of Jesus, His Son and mirror image allows and completes Perfect Justice also. I might note that I personally do not believe in Justice. The term justice is punitive and I do not accept the concept of a punitive God; it negates the concept of Perfect Love. I include the observation of justice simply to appease those who demand it.

CHAPTER 17

God, The Universe and Heaven, Man as God

§

WE HAVE OFTEN HEARD AND possibly used the phrase "temples of the Holy Spirit". That is a reference to the Holy Spirit living within us. While I accept without reservation the veracity of that statement, I suspect few if any have a valid, realistic concept of how that is. If we accept that the Holy Spirit (Will of God) is what drives (sustains and keeps perfect) each proton, neutron and electron, then it is obvious that the Holy Spirit not only resides in each of us humans, but in every gravid object in the universe. That would, of course, include all dissembled matter. I might digress, to recognize that scientists now believe that most (67%) of the universe is made up of what they call dark matter and dark energy. To date, no one has identified a specific dark matter particle, but work proceeds at a feverish pitch to find one. However, it seems clear in their concepts, that the universe has both light matter which we can readily recognize and dark matter which as yet we cannot. One could legitimately assume that, since God in *charge* of all, His Spirit resides in dark matter also.

Having established that the Holy Spirit is in all things, what happens when living things die? What is death anyway?? Death might be defined in various ways, but one simple explanation would be *cessation of respiration*. In the animal world, that generally would mean cessation of oxygen intake and metabolic activity. In the vegetable world that generally means cessation of carbon dioxide intake and cessation of photosynthesis. There are some bacteria (animals???) that respire without oxygen. In any event, with death comes the immediate beginning of the decomposition process; that is reducing the once living to its basic chemical components and eventual assimilation in other living or nonliving forms. What, then, happens to our being (soul; rationality)?

Most cultures accept that there is a *hereafter*, an afterlife of some sort. Some believe that they will be reincarnated as an animal or some other being. Others believe that only Homo sapiens, *so called rational beings*, will have the possibility of going to *heaven*, a *place* where they will see God. Some think of heaven as a "garden of paradise" where their bodies will be reunited with their soul and they will live perpetually in perfect happiness in God's presence.

We have often heard from *religious authorities* that heaven is a place where the blessed will "see God". If that is the case, and I am personally inclined to accept the concept that we will see God as He is, then the conclusion is obvious; WE WOULD BE GOD. That conclusion is reached in John's first letter where he proclaims "when we get to heaven we will see God as he is because we will be like Him (paraphrased). It would be impossible for any intellect to perceive God in His entirety and perfection without mirroring Him. I accept that God extended Himself into all things, and that all things are in Him and He is in all things. For the rational this reality materializes at death. You say, what about "dumb animals"? And I say, I don't know for sure anything, but I suspect they fit into the same category as we. We *all knowing, brilliant humans* presume to know that we are the only creatures capable of communicating with God simply because we can't communicate directly with so-called *dumb animals. It is entirely possible and even likely that animals communicate as well or better than we simply because their minds are not obscured by arrogance.* All things are of God, and therefore are God.

CHAPTER 18

Eternity

WHAT AN INTRIGUING TERM! It has so many uses with various implications. But, in general, the term seems to refer to a long time and sometimes to a very long time. For instance, we hear statements such as "it takes her an eternity to get ready", or "it blew him from here to eternity", or "he is forever and eternally late". The most important use of the word refers to an existence that has no beginning nor end. Therefore it cannot be measured in the usual units we call time. In fact it cannot be measured at all. One might ask then just how eternity comes to be.

The meaning of the word eternity is self-defining; where there is no time, there is no change. So then the word *eternity* would properly be defined as a state of existence without change. We have seen in previous chapters that we have defined God as a Perfect Rational Being. Since perfect demands no defect or deficiencies, a Perfect God never changes; hence He exists in Eternity.

How then do we and even all matter enter eternity? In order to comprehend the answer to this seemingly imponderable question, we must examine the very nature of our existence. I have pointed out in previous chapters that the entire universe is evil by virtue of its' universal selfishness. Selfishness demands change so that our desires, wishes, and greed might be fulfilled. I have noted that every existence, animate and inanimate operate in a continual and continuing state of selfishness. My contention is that God made it to be that way so He could be Perfect Love. TIME is a measure of change; where there is no change, there is no Time.

My faith is that Jesus inner being (soul) was/is God, equal to the Father. His appearance in the our tangible universe, at the time and place of its' occurrence, was the result of trillions of foregoing consequences. His genius intellect developed just as ours, but with much greater cognitive powers than any other human that ever existed. Definitely, He was "one of a kind". The man Jesus had physical needs just as all men and existences do. Because of that the man Jesus was selfish and thereby evil. You might cry out in horror that I have blasphemed against God. Not so. Do we not understand that the man Jesus was patterned with our complete nature as are all Homo sapiens? I believe that the man Jesus, just as we, was imbued with the Holy Spirit of God. The difference between Jesus and us is simple; Jesus was the only human being ever to recognize and accept the Will of God (the Holy Spirit) completely.

Once He accepted The Holy Will of God within Him, His spirit became evident; the same Spirit that permeates and sustains and makes perfect each and every tiny particle of God's creation. The Spirit exists in eternity because It is ever present and unchanging. The particulate matter which made up Jesus' body and every physical existence continues on *in time* because it is ever changing. The Christian bible and Christian Theology profess that Jesus' body arose from the dead and ascended into heaven. The unquestioned implication is then, that heaven is a physical place where body and soul reunite. Obviously no one knows anything for certain, but if that be the case, it would be mandatory for that body-soul existence to be in a perpetual inanimate state. If there were any motion or change, there would be no eternity.

The Christian belief suggests that heaven will be a perpetual Paradise; a place where people will be moving about, conversing with family and friends freely. I accept that their *Alice in Wonderland* concept "doesn't hold water". How then does our soul become eternal? One could ponder and speculate about this subject for *an eternity* with no conclusive argument forthcoming. However, my philosophy argues that since we "are made in the image and likeness of God", it necessarily follows that our *soul* is God. Again, many may consider me blasphemous. If that be the case then they don't mean what they say. My contention is that the Spirit of God (Holy Spirit [Will of God]) sustains every existence. He not only sustains every inanimate subatomic particle of which all matter is composed, but in the case of living matter, He is Our Soul. Since He has already freed us from guilt by His death, when our Soul (God) is liberated from its' physical home, it continues its' eternal existence as always.

The bottom line is this; selfishness = change and change = time. Where there is no selfishness, there is no time, only ETERNITY.

CHAPTER 19
But for the Grace of God, There Go I

§

How many times have we heard that statement, but, more importantly, how have we interpreted its' meaning? I suspect that many of us, deep down, felt somewhat smug in its' hearing; feeling maybe that somehow we were truly *blessed* by God while others were deliberately not blessed by God. Many of us probably felt that somehow we just lucked out and turned out reasonably well in our personality development. And, possibly, others didn't have a clue as to what the statement might mean as applied to themselves. My intention here is to explore the real meaning and significance of those words.

My general understanding of that statement is that somehow God has bestowed His grace (favor) on the speaker more so than the identified subject. Let us see if there is justification and truth in that assumption.

The development of the human psyche is extremely complicated and involves many factors. It is not my intent to elucidate each and every factor, but only enough to make the discussion understandable and meaningful. One might divide the psyche development into three stages; namely prenatal (intrauterine), postnatal infantile (age 0-5), and age of reason (5-6 to adulthood). Those divisions are all-inclusive and certainly could be subdivided into many categories; however, for our purposes here, they will suffice. The human psyche can be likened to a computer; it has an operating system (Microsoft windows, etc.), recent memory, and long-term memory; immeasurable storage and recall capabilities like computers. Different people have different storage and recall capabilities, and operate at different speeds depending upon the speed of their processor and the speed of information feed. In people, we may label these two quantities as IQ (native intelligence) and education.

Before either a computer or a human brain can function intelligently, it must have a basic Operating System installed. In humans that installation occurs mostly during the intrauterine and infantile-child stages of development. During those stages, we react to each stimulus applied to us and store that reaction information in our base operating system (subconscious). In that way we have available a ready-made response, should we ever again encounter any of those stimuli. Those, we call "learned response systems". Those systems are desirable, if they are legitimate (don't touch hot stove- it will burn and hurt), but, conversely, they may be very detrimental if erroneous (don't go into dark room- boogieman will get you). So, during our formative years, our subconscious is preprogramed with literally millions (billions) of ready-made responses; many of those are good and many are not so good. Most, if not all, of that programing comes from our environmental exposure, both intrauterine and extra-uterine, at a time when we are not yet equipped with a psyche which is able to reason correctly and make proper judgments. Consequently, we all are preprogramed with much false response information. As a result, we all, to some degree or another, are shackled with much baggage in our operating systems, which may interfere with our ability to function comfortably and efficiently in our lifetime. As I have stated previously, each and every happening of any kind is the direct consequence of billions of consequences that went before. Therefore, our preprograming directly influences our choices. If we are programed extremely poorly (massive socially unacceptable attitudes), and we never are exposed to influences directing our choices elsewhere, it is possible to continually make choices which ultimately lead us to accept, as good, Jeffrey Dahmer type activity and attitude. On the other hand, if our preprograming is more in line with reality, we have the opportunity to develop as socially acceptable people.

How then is it justified to make the statement "but for the grace of God, there go I"? Only if one believes that God plays favorites, or that

God rewards good and punishes bad (evil) [the belief of the Jews], could that statement be true. It is true that God created all the building blocks (PNE's) of the universe, but from there I accept that God has taken a *hands-off* attitude toward His creation other than keeping each of those particles perfect by His Holy Spirit (Will [Love]). It is not by God's direct intervention that we are what we are but purely by chance in His perfect universe. I have seen numerous people demonstrate a seemingly smug attitude about their status before God. They convey an attitude that since they go to church more than others, or that they pray more, or give more money to the church than others might, that, somehow, they become more acceptable (better) in God's eye. No doubt, in their eye, yes; in God's eye? I doubt it. Simply stated we are what we are by virtue of millions of events and consequences that we had to choose the *good* in; whether or not our choices were in fact good, they were always good in our opinion and therefore had to be accepted. That, of course, led to a perpetual state of "The Road Not Taken" in our lives. We always have to choose what seems to be the better, and that judgment is always based on the millions and millions of prior judgments. So maybe we should not be so smug in our attitude. It seems to me that an attitude of humility and gratitude toward others, rather than one of scorn and demeaning is in order.

The farther down the path of life a person goes, the more unlikely it is that he/she ever can be brought around to "the path not taken". That is why proper programing of our psyches in the formative stages is so critical. It is nearly impossible to bring an older adult around to the "path not taken". The only legitimate method of attempting such a maneuver that I am aware of is an in-depth psychoanalysis. That method allows an individual to *relive* one's early childhood and re-judge important decisions with an adult mind that were erroneously judged previously with an immature mind. That, indeed, may be of great benefit in alleviating major problems and subconscious misconceptions in one's life. However, it would be literally impossible to re-live one's entire life and thereby correct all of one's misjudgments; the time involved would amount to another lifetime, and, even if we had the time, the cost would be prohibitive for most. Suffice it to say, a limited superficial psychoanalysis would most likely benefit all.

In summary then, there appears to be no justification for anyone feeling more special than his/her neighbor in God's eye, no matter how vile a person he or she may seem. That conclusion is justified by Jesus' command to "love your neighbor as yourself". I submit to you that if we, as individuals, accepted that command personally, we would have neither time nor energy for "except for the grace of God, there go I." Loving your neighbor as yourself is a full time job indeed, and precludes any possibility of being more blessed or favored by God.

CHAPTER 20

Jesus (The Christ)

§

WHO WAS/IS JESUS? THAT QUESTION was pondered and argued for centuries, beginning even while He lived. The bible tells us He was the Son of God and the son of Mary by virtue of Mary's impregnation by the Holy Spirit. Could there be another more plausible explanation of His identity and derivation than the biblical version. I will attempt to offer such an explanation based on science and philosophy without, in any way, casting any negativity about His essence. He is the Son of God but, I will argue that point from a far different philosophical and scientific foundation than that depicted in the bible.

I begin my argument by asking you to recognize, as you read the bible, that Luke and, particularly, Matthew were Zealots of the highest order. They, obviously, were very conversant with the Old Testament writings, and being convinced that Jesus was truly the Messiah, they were *hell bent* on making all the prophetic predictions in the Old Testament come to *living fruition* in their writings about Him. They began by fabricating a genealogy of Jesus as stemming from the House of David through a foster father Joseph. Mary was from the House of Aaron, but because she had to be a "virgin", she could not be impregnated by a mortal man. I recognize there is some dispute about Mary's genealogy, but as far as I can determine, the majority recognize her lineage from Aaron. That mattered little to Luke and Matthew; a foster father *transmitted the blood line* just fine. Then there is the story of The Presentation of Jesus in the Temple 40 days after Jesus birth, followed by immediate return home, as told by Luke. In Matthew's *version*, we are presented with a completely different scenario involving a guiding star, astrologers from the East bringing Baby Jesus gifts, Herod's order for slaughter of innocents, but more importantly, the fleeing of the Holy Family to Egypt, where they remained possibly as long as 12 years. It is quite obvious that both of these stories cannot be true, and logic demands the possibility of neither being true. As one reads the various biblical accounts of the events in Jesus' life, one cannot help but notice the constant reminder that *such and such* happened "that the scriptures might be fulfilled". In other words, it seems to me there were continuing struggles among New Testament writers to make all of their perceived prophetic predictions come to life in their Jesus stories.

The stories surrounding John the Baptist and his cousin Jesus make it seem that they might hardly have known each other; that somehow, by inspirational knowledge, The Baptist knew that Jesus was savior even though they possibly had never met. Keep in mind; they were cousin, living in the same vicinity. To me it is inconceivable that two people with such *radical* ideas as they had would not have conversed at length about their *new philosophy* which differed so greatly from their Jewish tradition. I would suggest that their meeting in the Jordan, if it did indeed take place, was *staged*, so to speak, as their *coming out* party. In any event, my take is that the New Testament writers painted a picture filled with mystery, innuendo, secrecy, and above all, attempts at fulfilling the Old Testament predictions. Those few examples will suffice to accent the point

To make matters worse, their expectations of Jesus bore only fruits of disappointment. They were expecting Gods messenger to bring them news of a new paradise just for them, and that it was to be recreated immediately. They were stupefied to learn that their savior had to die, but they were reassured in Mark's gospel that He would return and restore the Kingdom before the present generation passed; such was their determination to make their interpretation of Old Testament statements come true. Of course, obviously nothing happened as predicted, and 2000 years later, we are waiting for God to *make good* on His promise.

Now, here is my take. First of all, I do not accept any of the *so called* prophetic predictions found in the Old Testament. I believe they were the Jews' imaginary wishful and egotistical way of interpreting the events in their lives. They knew no science, they had no appreciation of the universe as it really was, and more importantly, they humanized their God to the point of bargaining down to *the last penny* with Him. That's understandable, because their entire existence was based on a set of rules and regulations which Moses had convinced them had come directly from God. So, they felt obliged to bargain and work out an agreement, *covenant*, with God that *if they would do so and so, He would do such and such*. So imbued were they with this idea, that when Jesus came along, and being so convinced that He was the One, they felt compelled to make Him *fit the picture* or, better still, *make the picture fit Him*. Therein lays one of the principal bases for the many, many discrepancies found in the bible. Each writer *flavored* the story to his own liking. But not one of them except possibly Paul could admit to the complete divinity (equality with the Father) of Jesus. Neither, did anyone of them seemingly have a clear cut notion of, or about, The Holy Spirit.

I will be the first to admit that I know nothing with absolute certainty, and I would also readily admit to ignorance regarding God's intentions. However, since presumably, humans are rational beings, patterned after the rationality of God, it is then rational to assume that God would think and act rationally in all respects. I have explained in previous writings that each and every event in this universe is a direct consequence of prior events; each and every event is perfect in itself and follows the perfect rationality of God's creation, "P, N, E's".

With that in mind, the so called Virgin Birth is highly unlikely. In order for that to happen, God would have to change His nature. From a rational standpoint, since God is perfect, change is impossible. I will digress to note that one zealous defender of the virgin birth asserted that the Holy Spirit impregnated Mary and that all his DNA was derived from Mary. If that be the case, Jesus would have been a half clone of Mary, most likely not possible of sustaining life. If God had miraculously duplicated Mary's DNA, Jesus would have been an exact clone of Mary.

I would propose that Joseph was the natural father of Jesus. That would, of course, by chance, make him from the House of David. Also, and more importantly, it is highly likely that Jesus was a *child prodigy*. In which case, he would have studied and understood the scriptures at a very young age much better than the wisest old sages. Being extremely versed in biblical understanding would explain the story of His remaining behind and teaching the astonished elders in the temple at the age of twelve

He knew a messiah was to come. His extreme insight into the relationship of God to the universe (God is in everything and everything is in God) led him to understand that His Spirit and the Father's Spirit were one. He undoubtedly recognized the *universal evil of selfishness* because all his teachings and suggestions, as far as we can determine, revolved around that theme. Recognizing that this universally evil universe had been created by His Father, and understanding that He and His Father must be Perfect Love, He saw Himself as Son Of God, the Sacrificial Lamb, Who must *pay the price* of Perfect Love and Perfect Justice. Jesus insight, understanding and faith would have led Him to that conclusion.

I believe with all my humble intellectual power, endowed in me by my creator, Almighty and Perfect God, that this scientific and philosophical explanation of Jesus and the events surrounding His life are rational in every respect. I graciously welcome any and all, scientific, logical and philosophical rebuttal (discussion) regarding this subject.

CHAPTER 21

Why Jesus Had to Die

§

ONE OBVIOUS REASON FOR JESUS' death was to be *Perfect love*; to accept without conditions the entire evil (selfish) universe which He had created. The less obvious but necessary reason for His death was to accept the *Perfect Justice* sentence demanded by the act of such creation. That singular act of complete submission and acceptance of the Father's Will completed the requirements of God's perfection.

One might reasonably question the suggestion that God could do or cause to be done anything evil. We are so imbued with the idea that evil pertains to violating the Ten Commandments that we fail to realize that all commandment breaches of any kind are summed up in one evil, *selfishness*. Jesus, the man, was selfish. He had to eat, sleep, eliminate, be clothed and sheltered, and communicate, just as all living creatures do. All these activities are necessarily directed at self, and by their very nature are evil because they put self before others. As I have noted before, God created the entire universe of selfish existences, both animate and inanimate. Why He chose that method of executing (demonstrating) His Perfection is anyone's guess, but the fact remains, He did.

Having said that, what does it mean for you and me? If we accept the oft heard clichés of 1-we are made in the image and likeness of God and 2-we are temples of the Holy Spirit, then I suspect that somehow, when our physical bodies are swept away, what will be left is God. That may sound egotistical and blasphemous, but I humbly ask the question, *how else can it be?* This concept begs directly of the nature of our eternal existence and directly confronts the concept of Purgatory.

The concept of Purgatory demands a *time of punishment* for our sinfulness before admission into heaven is possible. Even though God has forgiven us, we still have to *expiate the stain* of our sin by spending time in a place of torment. That idea is completely contradictory to the concept of eternity being a state of being where there is no change. Time is a measure of change, and since the idea of Purgatory involves time and change, it violates two primary principles of logic.

The Judeo-Christian tradition has always taught that eternal heaven was a *place* where people will be reunited, greet, converse, have emotional exchange and be perpetually and perfectly happy. They seemingly have interpreted Jesus' remarks, "in My Father's house there are many mansions" and "I go to prepare a place for you", to mean there are different *levels* of *happiness*. We are lead to believe that the more we sacrifice and do good works, the *high*er place we will get in heaven. Did it ever occur to anyone that such ideation perpetuates our sinfulness (evil=selfishness) right into heaven? If the concept of heaven as being a place or state of *perfect happiness* applies, is it possible to be more happy than *perfectly* happy? My sense of logic says "no". If Jesus truly did die for our salvation; *my only Faith is that He did*; then it follows that our eternal happiness is guaranteed with no greater or lesser degree for anyone.

The Jews conjured up an idea that they were the "chosen" people of God to His "abandonment" of all others. They had a pact (covenant) with God that He would provide for them through *thick and thin*. They believed that when they prospered it was because they found favor with God, and conversely, when things went bad in their lives, it was because God was punishing them for their evil doings. They recognized that their ancestors Adam and Eve, who were created into Paradise, had sinned against God, and therefore had been banished from Paradise along with all their progeny. They knew from this that they were destined to a life of toil on this earth, but if they could keep God's favor they would be very successful. They measured success largely by the size of their animal flocks, by the fertility of their brood stock wife to give them many sons, and by the grandeur of their domiciles. As time progressed they were drawn into captive slavery of the Egyptians prompted by a great famine. While there, they were exposed to the Egyptian ritual of baptismal cleansing. Finally, Moses who was wanted for murder rose to power among his countrymen and demanded freedom from the slavery. God had promised Moses a land of "milk and honey". When the Pharaoh refused to release them, God sent 10 plagues upon the Egyptians, prompting the Pharaoh to reconsider and release the Israelites.

The Israelites escaped but Moses, himself, never reached the Promised Land because he doubted Gods power. However, God protected the Israelites from their enemies by helping them slaughter many enemy assailants. In the course of due time, the Israelites established 12 tribes and inhabited the land. Kings came and went; events great and small occurred. Before Moses passed on, God gave him the 10 commandments. Also God established a new covenant with the Israelites and from then on they carried God around in *The Arc of the Covenant*. The new covenant was that God would never again abandon them and moreover he would send a Messiah to reestablish The Kingdom, *a new paradise here on earth just for them.*

When Jesus appeared and began preaching the *good news* of God's love and forgiveness of one another, it was a shock and surprise to the Jews who were programed with a philosophy of "an eye for an eye and a tooth for a tooth". Many also took exception to that teaching and considered it heresy and a threat to their religion. The boiling point was reached when Jesus proclaimed to them that He was the Messiah for whom they had been waiting. In no way did He *fill the bill* of the Messiah King they had been expecting, and when they questioned Him about when He was going to restore the Kingdom, Jesus replied to them, "the Kingdom of God is spread out all over the earth about you and you don't recognize it". This caused them extreme quandary. However when He told them that first He had to die, they did not understand at all. When His crucifixion and death finally took place, they were bewildered, and dismayed. Supposedly, Jesus told them that he would rise on the 3rd day, but they didn't believe Him. The gospel stories depict Jesus appearing several times to the apostles and holy women. They also depict Jesus final words and Ascension to Heaven.

The early writer Paul was so imbued with the idea that Jesus was coming right back to set up Paradise again, that he scolded everyone severely for leading a normal life of working, getting married etc., demanding that those activities were a waste of time. Mark's gospel quotes Jesus as saying that all of the "end time" events, including the second coming, would take place within a generation (40 years). History clearly shows all of this to be false; it is now near 2000 years and still no coming. What does that mean?

What it means to me is this. With my understanding of God as a Perfect Rational Being that exists in a *perfect state of unchanging eternity*, and knowing how the Jews were so imbued with the idea of a *second paradise*, the early writers and story tellers undoubtedly concocted those stories of resurrection, apparitions and ascension to satisfy their prejudicial convictions. Everywhere in the gospels, *such and such* happens to fulfill a prophecy in the Old Testament. The Jews had to make their *Fairy Tale* come true. The God of the Jews was human like; He sat on a throne; His Son sat at his right hand. This God of theirs who made a universe so large and complicated that no one can begin to comprehend it is bending to their will. They never once seized upon the idea that Gods Will is perfect and unchangeable. They could not accept Jesus telling them at the last supper that the bread and wine He held in his sacred hands were part of His perpetual existence as was everything else in this universe. They did not want a God that was independent from them. They never once considered *accepting* God's will; all they wanted was to *control* God's will.

The Christian Jews, who were the most numerous factions when Constantine called the council of Nicaea, had developed a religious ritual right out of the Israelite *play book*. They had Baptism, and they had sacrifice. They conveniently took Jesus' words "this is My body and My blood", and Jesus command for them to *remember that when they ate*, to mean that they were *recreating* Jesus each time they said those words. I believe that Jesus was telling them to recognize that everything was His body and blood; *He is in all things and all things are in Him.*

With that in mind, I do not accept that Jesus' resurrection and ascension were necessary or that they took place. In order for those events to have happen, God would have been required to *change His nature* as I understand it, and since God is perfect and unchangeable, that was not possible.

CHAPTER 22
Creeds Versus The Bible

CHRISTIANS, WORLDWIDE, ARE CATECHIZED BY two major creeds, the Apostles Creed and the Nicene Creed. Each creed is used by different denominations to a varying degree, and with somewhat different wording, depending upon time of year or immediate circumstance. My intent is not to elucidate every twist and turn in the evolutionary development of these two documents, but to show the apparent constant confusion and lack of understanding about the nature of God, Jesus, and the Holy Spirit. Also, I will show a complete contradiction of Luke's gospel by the Apostles Creed.

The Apostles Creed apparently emanated from an earlier document known as The Old Roman Symbol. The first mention of the term Apostles Creed was in 390 AD. The version we have today seems to have first appeared AD 715-750. In any event the creed clearly states that Jesus "descended into hell and arose again on the third day". When researching the meaning of the statement "He descended into hell", one is left bewildered. No commentator has a clear, rational explanation of the term. Yet it is still used on a regular basis by Western Churches. Reportedly, Eastern Churches have abandoned its' use.

The Nicaean Creed has a somewhat similar history; being formulated piecemeal for centuries. It was begun during the first council of Nicaea in AD 325 and revised and expanded at the first council of Constantinople in 381. Reportedly multiple revisions have been published over the centuries. The Roman Catholic Church in The United States adopted the latest revision in 2011. At least ten or more versions of this creed are used by different Western and Eastern Orthodox Churches.

So, what does all that mean? What it means to me is the clear-cut fact that, seemingly, no one in Jesus' time, nor since, has understood Jesus' real identity. I have offered a clear, philosophically sound, explanation of His true identity and purpose.

A few days ago, while driving to my farm in the country, I noticed three bare wooden crosses standing in front of a small country church. I have passed by those crossed hundreds of times over the years, but this time was different. I thought of Jesus hanging on His cross with the two insurgents on either side. I remembered Luke's description of Jesus' conversation with them. One of them asked Jesus to remember him when He entered into His kingdom, and Jesus' reply, "this day thou shalt be with Me in paradise". Suddenly it struck me; the Apostles Creed says Jesus descended into hell for three days upon His death. WHAT A CONTRADICTION! WHAT ARE WE TO BELIEVE?

Does that leave any doubt about the ignorance and confusion of our early church leaders, theology developers, and writers? Personally, I am shocked and appalled at the idiotic philosophy proposed and imposed on us, literally by them all. As stated many time before, each writer (teacher) tried desperately to make Jesus fit the mold of Old Testament writings. They all failed. What is even more disheartening; we are still shackled by that total nonsense. Any rational mind which allows itself the freedom of clear thinking should reach the same conclusion as I. That may sound egotistical, but I humbly ask for your philosophically sound and logical rebuttal.

CHAPTER 23

Eucharist

LITERALLY TRANSLATED, THE WORD EUCHARIST means *thanksgiving*. With that understanding, how did the Eucharistic meal suggested by Jesus become a *sacrificial* event? Early church history regarding that subject is scant if nonexistent. There are many references to "breaking the bread" to be found but none regarding it as a sacrificial event. So why is it that way in Catholic liturgy? I certainly would be the first to admit my ignorance on this subject first hand. However, having rather extensive knowledge about the history of sacrificial liturgies practiced in pre-Christian eras would suggest a reasonable answer to the question.

In reviewing pre-Christian religious rituals one finds sacrificial offerings of one kind or another were the norm for the purpose of appeasing the gods and later on by the Jews for purpose of appeasing God for their sins. In some instances human sacrifices were the norm. Most, however, involved other animal or produce offerings with the specific animal and/or amount being determined by the gravity of the need. Plainly then, most, if not all people, were *programed* to expect sacrifice of one kind or another as part of their religious experience. We have inference from various sources how converts to a *way of thinking* were recruited by allowing some of their rituals to be included in their new religious life. It would seem certain that the Jews, after being in captivity of the Egyptians, adopted some aspects of the Egyptian baptismal and sacrificial rites. That aspect of Jewish ritual made it easier to entice nearby prospective pagan converts. However there seems to exist again this threading of lack of agreement and clear understanding of Christian (Catholic) doctrine regarding that subject. The first *official* time I can find for use of the term Eucharistic Sacrifice was an edict from Pope Gregory the Great (604). The Council of Trent 1542 officially reiterated doctrine.

It is quite obvious to me that there was mass confusion about who Jesus really was. In addition, there was suspicion about the meaning of His Last Supper words, "this is My body and blood", paraphrased; John didn't even mention them in his gospel. So, given the fact that converts were mandated and ritual sacrifice was an integral part of every person's life (Jew and non-Jew alike), it is highly likely that those in charge found it *desirable and necessary* to incorporate sacrifice into their *New Ritual* in order to attract converts. Nowhere in the gospel writings, does Jesus say "do his as a sacrificial offering to me". What He does say is "do this in memory of Me". My interpretation of those words, as explained elsewhere, is that Jesus was telling them that *His Spirit is in all things and all things are in Him*, and He was reminding them to be ever aware of that fact, and to be forever thankful for His presence and sacrifice for their (our) salvation.

The Church has conveniently translated those words as a *mandate of power* on its part to *re create* Jesus as a sacrificial offering. My thesis is that the Spirit of God permeates each quantum of energy in the universe; He therefore cannot be more in one place than another. His Spirit already is and always is in everything. In that sense everything should be considered Eucharist, *thanksgiving to God for His Perfection*.

Also, when one peruses the literature regarding that subject, it seems that all of the writers busy themselves defining and defending the Churches position on Eucharist, rather than answering the question, "when did the term's use officially begin". It seems that the *indoctrinated* seldom saw fit to question anything (in my lifetime, questions were never allowed). Some famous Greek philosopher once said "question everything". My suspicion as to why the Church forbade questions is because seldom did they have a unified answer. Any good teacher who knows the answer is usually eager to share that knowledge. *If one doesn't know (have) the answers, questions are seldom welcomed.*

CHAPTER 24

The Soul

THE HUMAN SOUL IS ONE of the most frequently mentioned entities when matters of religion or spirituality are being discussed. I suspect, without being able to prove, that I have heard the term several million time. However, in spite of its' frequent use, I don't recall ever once hearing a suitable definition of the human soul. We hear terms such as *the soul, our soul, her soul, his soul, poor soul, everlasting soul, black soul, stained soul, pure soul, lost soul,* etc., but never do we hear a definitive description or definition of a soul. What then is the essence of a (the) soul?

In order to get a glimpse into the understanding of the term soul, we need only to look no farther than the *human* Jesus. My contention is that God, being perfect, ordained all existence from eternity. Being such means that no change is possible. That is to say that each and every occurrence in God's existence has an eternal ordination and not subject to change. Even God, being perfect, cannot change. His Will is eternal. The concept of a "virgin birth" denies and negates God's perfection and therefore is impossible.

Undoubtedly, Jesus was a human genius. If we can garner anything from the Bible, that fact seems clear. He obviously was more conversant with, and had better insight into, Old Testament scriptures than any of the wisest sages of His time. Most importantly, Jesus recognized that His inner being (soul), as well as the inner being of all existences, mirrored the being of their Creator. He also saw and recognized the universal evil of *selfishness* in all existences. He undoubtedly understood the concept of a

Perfect God, which includes, of course, Perfect Love. He understood that *active Perfect Love* demanded a *love target equal to the capacity of the Lover, Almighty God*. What better love (acceptance) target than an entire eternal existence of evil (selfishness) which He, Himself, had created?

Even though Jesus knew His soul mirrored God, as brilliant as he was, he freely admitted his inequality with God on a knowledge basis; his material intellect in no way equaled God's. However, Jesus' recognized that God must pay the price (accept) all the evil which He had created. He readily concluded, that since he was the only one to visualize those facts, he had to be the Messiah. His knowledge of that understanding would have lead him to know and accept that his soul, mirroring God's, must pay the price of "Perfect Love". He did so willingly, but with great human fear and trepidation. So what does that have to do with defining "the soul"? Everything, and we call it essence.

Essence is that quality which makes something what it basically is. Accidents are those qualities which make something an individual version of what it is. For instance, the essence of a table is its' "tableness"; its' accidents are what make it a specific table; three legged, four legged, black, dull, shiny, square, round, etc. So it is with the soul. Each soul mirrors the soul (Perfect Nature) of Eternal God. That Nature cannot be seen in its present cloak of selfishness (accidents) applied to each and every existence by God Himself. When all entities, animate or inanimate, cease to be, their accidents will be removed and their essence, God, will remain forever as always.

Whoever wrote John's first letter recognized that fact. He states flatly that when we get to heaven, we will see God as he is, because we will be like Him (paraphrased).

So what does all that mean regarding our relationship with God? What it means to me is the following:

Each entity in existence is created with the basic nature (essence) of God,

Each entity is endowed with its own individual set of characteristics (accidents) which imparts its selfishness (evil),

Jesus died to be Perfect Love and thereby removed the shroud of shame and guilt from everything,

The only legitimate prayer is Thanksgiving to God for our existence, for our sustenance, and for our eternal salvation and life,

There is no legitimate sacrifice,

There is no need nor justification for organized religion,

The only commandments are Love God and neighbor as much as possible,

The only justifiable "religious" ministry is teaching and promulgating those two principles,

Every other question in our existence is a matter of civil consideration and regulation.

CHAPTER 25
Marriage and Sex

IT IS DOUBTFUL THAT MANY Christians are conversant with the history of marriage. The reason for that is clear. Christians are so indoctrinated that few mental queries arise regarding their beliefs. They are led by skillful inference and instructional neglect to believe that contemporary attitudes and ceremonies have been the norm for centuries. Most would be shocked to learn of the real history of marriage; that is to say that the way things are now is not the way they were in early Jewish and Christian eras.

My intention here is not to elucidate every twist and turn in the development of Church philosophy concerning matrimony. It is, however, to highlight the salient changes that have taken place over the last 2500 years, and to show that those changes represent a complete about-face regarding the validity and advisability of marriage union. More importantly, I will demonstrate the complete and absolute disregard for Jesus' teachings and attitude toward marriage. I will also show the early church's near total disdain of marriage and, more importantly, its total abhorrence of sex in any form.

The irrationality espoused by the early Church is astonishing but understandable when one considers Paul's teaching. It is precisely Paul's belief and insistence that the *second coming of Christ* was eminent, that leads me to accept one of two possible conditions regarding Paul's understanding of Christianity. Either Paul has been misrepresented in our current copy of the bible or he was beset by an overwhelming emotional experience which he interpreted otherwise.

If our current version of the bible represents his original writing, it can rightly be assumed that he was grossly misinformed. If he truly had obtained his information directly from Jesus there would have been no misunderstanding about the timing of *second coming*. It seems to me that another source of Paul's indoctrination is likely; namely, from those whom he persecuted. Remember, by the time Paul began his persecuting activity against the Jesus followers, Jesus had been dead for possibly several years. By that time, there were, undoubtedly, many wishful thinkers and believers who thought Jesus was coming right back, and, because of this hope and belief, they were willing to endure whatever insult and back-thrashing Paul hurled at them. They wanted to be part of Jesus' grand return. Obviously Paul was a very determined, but equally intelligent man. It is likely that he became inquisitive about the beliefs of those whom he persecuted and was instructed by them about the nature and activities of Jesus. Since there was no uniform understanding of Jesus even by His apostles, there would have been all sorts of misrepresentations of factual Jesus among the faithful. I strongly suspect this was the source of Paul's information.

It is a very plausible idea to accept that Paul's sudden realization that, in reality, he was persecuting Jesus, Himself, frightened him into an extreme emotional hysteria, which he interpreted as a direct encounter with Jesus. Whatever the reason, it is quite obvious that Paul's teaching was in error as was his resultant scorning of marriage; his reasoning was correct but his premises were wrong. Therefore his conclusions had to be wrong.

In the Jewish tradition, marriage was an arranged event. A man's daughter was a liability. In order to rid himself of her, he must "cough up" a sizeable chunk of his wealth as a dowry. That was the price he had to pay a man to accept her as his wife. It really represented her inheritance. That union (marriage) was a contractual civil event and in no way a spiritual religious occasion. A breech of that contract through Mosaic Law became known as "sin". Adultery was a violation of a man's civil rights and was punishable by death through stoning. A woman had little if any rights. Her principle purpose was as a domestic slave and *brood sow*. She was a man's property. The irony here is that even though the man had to be paid to take a woman, once she became his property, he guarded her jealously and his ownership was guaranteed by Mosaic Law.

Jesus saw the gross injustices heaped upon women and reportedly made a concerted effort to correct those inequities. Our current version of the bible (correctly or incorrectly) tells us Jesus refused to condemn the harlot, Mary Magdalene, when she was caught in adultery and was brought before Jesus for a death sentence by stoning; neither would he condemn the Samaritan woman "at the well" who had multiple husbands. Jesus knew the law but, in His wisdom, He also knew that attempting to change it could and would be lethal for Himself. He knew He had to die but the timing was not yet right; he still had to convince his illiterate companions of His real identity which they had not yet grasped. He still had to instill into their biased intellects the true nature of God, His relationship to God and God's relationship to the entire universe. In spite of that fact, Jesus was determined to elucidate and correct those injustices.

His insight made Himself aware that His soul and every soul mirrored their Creator, and with that in mind, there was no justification for inequality of the sexes. More importantly, he recognized that there was no justification for demonizing the natural instincts which he had instilled in all living things. Since He could not physically protect those women, His admonition to both of them to "go and sin no more" was undoubtedly intended as advice for their own protection, which He could not afford them.

From the time of Jesus' death until now, the Church has been in a constant state of flux formulating, promulgating, mandating, and pontificating attitudes, rules and regulations regarding sex and marriage. Their flip-flopping attitude toward marriage and sex from Paul's day until now is unbelievably hypocritical. Those attitudes could and probably would be accepted as understandable by the faithful were it not for the Church's continued profession of absolute Magisterium. If they were wrong then, how can we know they are correct now? The answer is simple; we can't.

Paul, the earliest Christian writer stated flatly that virginity and celibacy were the admirable virtues. Marriage was a waste of time and energy and a distraction from the preparation for the eminent return of The Savior. Marriage was regrettably acceptable only if a *man* could not *contain* himself; the grossest degradation of women. They were reduce to mere collecting vessels for men's semen.

As time progressed, a philosophy was developed which avowed sex under any circumstance to be bad. Women, by their very existence were considered by the church to be intrinsically evil and unworthy. They carried all the enticement for evil in men. In other words, it was an accepted principle that, were it not for women, men would not be tempted to sin sexually. What a cop-out. The all- knowing hierarchy (men) were basically exonerated from sex sin by the mere existence of evil women. DOES THE ADAM AND EVE STORY SOUND FAMILIAR?

Consequently, a premium was placed on virginity in women. It became her most prized possession and attribute. The man who robbed a woman of her virginity wrought her wrath forever. According to Taylor, there was a time in church history when the priest who witnessed the ceremony was the first to copulate with the bride. Later on it became the custom for all the men in the bridal party to have sex with the bride before the husband had his turn. The logic here was that the husband would not have to bear the blame for stealing his wife's virginity.

Sex was so abhorrent and women so contaminated with "sex smells" that for centuries weddings were not allowed inside the church building. They were presided over by the local priest but were done either at the church door or in the church courtyard. Under the best of considerations, marriage was grudgingly allowed and tolerated. Gradually it became clear that Paul's analysis of the second coming was foolish. The Church realized that if sexual contact between male and female was not allowed, the human race would become extinct.

In spite of that realization, sex in itself remained a grave but necessary evil. It was so evil that it basically must be performed in a vacuum of consciousness and emotion. That is to say that *NO* pleasure of any king was allowed.

During the Inquisition, anyone observed or simply accused of experiencing pleasure during the sex act would automatically be burned at the stake. So determined was the church of the dangers of sex that intercourse on a suspended bed (that is anywhere except on the ground) would incur the same immediate fate, death by fire. The reason for that prohibition was simple; the vibrations and shaking created by copulation on a bed might cause the earth to fall off its supports and tumble into the netherworld below. That stipulation and resultant punishment persisted three years after Vasco de Gama sailed around the earth proving the earth to be round; such was the lunacy of the hierarchy.

I have been unable to determine the exact inception date that weddings were allowed inside church buildings. As best I can determine, there was no explicit date. Likely, the custom started as a local aberration and gradually spread to other communities. However history does tell us when the Church decided it was pragmatic to declare marriage a sacrament. In the year 1184 marriage was first declared a sacrament of the church but not equal to the others sacraments.

Since that time we have seen a litany of directives regarding marriage, divorce, birth control, and literally anything and everything having to do with sex, marriage and procreation. So now we have reached the point that the Church driven by fear of losing control of the populace has tightened the reins on every minute aspect of anything sexual.

No longer can they torment, terrorize, and vaporize people physically. They do it *mentally and emotionally*, a much worse sentence. The physical pain and torment imposed during the inquisition and before, albeit horrible, were temporary; the mental and emotional agony mandated now lasts a lifetime. I am certain that the extreme guilt and resultant anxiety generated by the attempted repression of God-given sexual instincts mandated by the Church are directly responsible for the majority of emotional and mental illness witnessed in Christians today and throughout history.

Taylor described Medieval Europe as one giant "insane asylum". Even when I was a child in the 1930's and '40's, there was a prohibition against married couples having sex the night before receiving communion the next morning; such was the church's phobia of sex. Preaching such a deranged attitude toward a perfectly normal activity certainly would create extreme guilt and anxiety among the faithful with resultant severe emotional and mental derangement. As a physician, I have personally witnessed that exact scenario innumerable times.

There are other clandestine motives the church has exhibited just in my lifetime. In the diocese of Owensboro, Ky., it was mandatory under pain of mortal sin or excommunication that every Catholic child and adult attend a Catholic educational institution. In 1950, when one of my older brothers returned home from military service, he intended to live at home with our parents, and attend Murray State University. Our local priest informed my parents that they would be *excommunicated* if they allowed my brother to live in their home while attending a secular university. Rather than cause emotional strain on our parents, my brother moved to Scottsdale, Az., where he lived with another brother while attending Arizona State University.

The motivation behind such ridiculous regulations seems clear and it doesn't have to do with spirituality. It does have to do with the *almighty dollar*. The more indoctrinated we are, the less likely we are to leave the church. The more people going to church, the fuller the collection basket.

That same motivation undoubtedly drives the irrational probation against artificial birth control. The more kids, the merrier; more empire building money.

Strangely, the prohibition of attending secular schools was lifted. As the cost of education increased, the cost of operating schools increased. Tuitions went higher and Catholics bolted Catholic schools in favor of secular schools. That meant churches had to spend their *precious money* to keep the doors open; an unthinkable idea. Many people left the church rather than face ridicule from parishioners and pastors alike. That, of course, reduced incomes more. All of a sudden, catholic schools began closing like wildfire nationwide.

There again, the Catholic mandate (moral authority) bowed to the almighty dollar. Even as I speak, our current pope Francis has made many "politically correct" statements and declarations to help stem the tide of efflux from the church. One of the most notable paraphrased; "no rules have changed, we just got to stop talking about them". And, we must show more "mercy"; "priests can give absolution to women who have had an abortion". Divorced people who remarry outside the church without an annulment can now receive the sacraments. Now, if those rules were absolute and punishable by damnation to eternal hell heretofore, *how is possible that all of a sudden they now are not?*

So to summarize, we see an ignorant, egotistical, selfish, superstitious Church defying Jesus by defaming and abusing women and ultimately men. Jesus in His union with God and Their Holy Spirit created all living things with innate impulses aimed at insuring propagation of the species "come hell or high water". The Church has steadfastly operated on a self-serving, superstitious set of principles derived from the Old Testament, all of which have led to the utter detriment of mankind. The Church has been overtly and completely wrong about every aspect of human existence since Jesus' death. And they tell us they have MAGESTERIUM?

CHAPTER 26

Love Versus Mercy

§

POPE FRANCIS RECENTLY PROCLAIMED A "year of Mercy" in the Catholic Church. Just what does the term "mercy" mean? By any reasonable definition, it infers a sense of *guilt with need for punishment* on the part of the recipient. It implies without doubt a sense of authority, superiority and ultimate control over one's fate; in this particular case as in all cases in the Catholic Church, ultimate, total control over our eternal fate; "heaven or hell". The term Mercy in the Catholic Church always indicates and dictates an overt authoritarian attitude toward its subjects. The Church totally ignores and seemingly abhors the concept of love. IT always implies a sense of extreme superiority over its' guilty subjects.

In previous chapters, we have discussed endlessly the concept of love. Simply put "one more time", as Jesus not only taught us but showed us endlessly, in no uncertain terms, that true love "is acceptance without *guilt". Jesus recognized the evil (selfishness) of the entire universe which He, Himself had created.* He recognized there could be no GUILT if we were not responsible for our selfishness which He had created in us, and in all things, so that His universe could function "In time" as He ordained. For that reason, He offered and gave His own life that our selfishness could be forgiven through a Perfect Act of Love by Him without any implication of Guilt. Certainly, then, no Mercy is implied nor mandated.

I would hasten to encourage Pope Francis to proclaim, rather than a "year of mercy", *"AN ETERNITY OF LOVE "*. Of course, this will not and cannot happen for one simple reason; Doing so would mean loss of all authority by the church; *not a chance of that happening.*

I should note here a near state of panic and angst among church leaders over the loss of membership particularly among young people. The Church is so near sighted, they seem not to understand why. The WHY is very, very, simple. When one takes very young innocent children and bewilders them with an idiotic idea that *they inherited an inborn state of hopeless evil* from some mythical characters who supposedly lived, thousands of years ago, their personalities are changed forever. They are taught that all of a sudden they went from being mentally and emotionally healthy children to being sinners who are on trial for the rest of their natural lives and even thereafter. No matter what they do or say, their *salvation* can come only through pleading and begging God to accept them through forgiveness mediated by the Church. They are taught that the God who created them, has put them on trial for their salvation from the *everlasting burning fires of hell* until the day of "last Judgement", and all because of the so-called sin of two mythical characters, Adam and Eve who supposedly lived thousands of years ago. Incessant prayer and strict adherence to the exact teachings of the church are their only chance of escape from eternal damnation. The rules imposed by the church are irrational in many instances, particularly regarding family planning. Since most people are rational and logical, they understand that the church's stance is unreasonable and illogical; so they simply ignore the dictums of the church. They immediately are ostracized because of their obtrusiveness. Since they simply find no solace or help from the church they quit attending.

Today's Gospel reading of the Prodigal son illustrates my point exactly. The church would have us believe that the father showed mercy to his son. However, nothing farther from the truth could be possible. If the father's reaction had been one of mercy he might have presented the following-like scenario; "Well son you may come home but you must tend the sheep and swine and eat whatever leftovers fall from my table". In other words, you must be punished before I will take you back. Ill treat you as an unimportant animal for a time. But that was not the case. The father threw his arms around his son in complete love and acceptance without condition of any kind, and with admonition to standers-by; hasten, put a fine robe on his back, a ring on his finger, sandals on his feet, and a crown on his head. My son who was lost is found and I am so happy and I ACCEPT him back in a complete act of LOVE (paraphrased). This is the problem with the Church. They are in control. They hold the KEYS TO THE KINGDOM in their hands. "You will do as we say or ELSE". We will distribute MERCY as we see fit. We never distribute LOVE. Only Jesus distributed Love and His commands and teaching have been completely ignored by the church. And for what reason? MONEY, POWER, CONTROL. And they wonder; "WHERE HAVE THE FAITHFUL GONE'?

CHAPTER 27

Free Will

§

How many thousand (million) of times have we heard/used the term *free will*. Thomas Aquinas elucidated the concept of free will, from his perspective, in great depth and length. His argument pits the information gathering Intellect against the all-powerful acting Will. His basic understanding seems to be grounded in what he accepted as the totally binding morality of the 10 commandments somehow intertwined with Natural Law. He saw the human intellect as being able to discern good from bad mostly on a moral level. Had he addressed the issue from a natural level, it is possible that some of his conclusions might have been different. He extrapolated ad nauseam the moral (sin) implications of every infraction of both moral and natural law. His basic mistake was in thinking that the will operates independently of the intellect. My contention is that there is no such thing as free will. Let us examine both concepts.

Aquinas View:

- Intellect collects information
- Intellect determines which is good (desirable) and which is bad (undesirable)
- Inters Will: Independently, Will decides which to select
    - Sometimes it selects good
        - If it selects good, there is no problem, and we gain merit and a potential higher place in heaven.

- Sometimes it selects bad (sin)
  - If it selects sin, then we are immediately shackled with guilt and mandated punishment of degree equal to the sin.

My View

- Intellect collects and analyzes information
- It determines which is good (desirable) and which is bad (undesirable)
- Inters Will: My contention is that the will does not and cannot operate independently of intellect, It is *duty bound* to choose (accept, love, spiritually permeate) whatever the intellect presents as good (desirable).

What Aquinas and moralists have confused with free Will is their failure to understand that it is impossible for a rational intellect (Will) to choose what it perceives as bad (undesirable). While the intellect may, in fact, perceive as good what others might consider bad (sinful, undesirable), it still chooses what *it* considers good. It is easy to see, then, that the Will does not and cannot operate independently of the intellect. Likewise it is never free to choose what the intellect determines to be bad. The Will is the *executive arm* of the intellect and must follow orders precisely. In an irrational (insane, psychotic) intellect, bad would frequently and consistently be chosen because of the intellect's inability to discern good and bad. There are implications generated by this concept, not the least of which is an understanding of illegal activity and the legitimate ideology of dealing with it. Briefly, my contention is that people, truly, are not *guilty of crimes per-primum*: as such our remedy should never be in the order of punishment (an eye for an eye), but in the order of protecting society from an abusive individual who sees as good his abusive activity, coupled with an intensive effort at rehabilitating such individuals; truly, an extensive conversation for another day, but not the least bit less important.

CHAPTER 28

Free Will and the Legal System

§

THE LEGAL SYSTEM IN THE U.S. and much of the free world is tied directly to the concept of "free Will". We, as a society, have been so brainwashed by so-called Judea-Christian moral values that seemingly, we cannot find a rational course of action for dealing with criminals. Because of our biased teaching regarding free will and morality, and taking a page directly from the Jewish playbook of "an eye for an eye---", we are unable to recognize the fundamental flaw in our system. Law breakers (criminals) are not so because they were born that way. They are who they are by way of personality development, which, as I have explained before, begins in utero. One has only to read and comprehend the meaning of the great poet Robert Frost's poem, "The Road Not Taken", to begin an understanding of how our personalities develop. When we are pre-programmed correctly, and are fortunate enough to get pointed down the desirable path, then our personality development qualifies us to exist and function in society with minimal legal difficulties. However, if we are less fortunate, and become the byproduct of poor preprograming with eventual wandering down the wrong path, then we become societal misfits in some degree or another.

The moment we breach any law, civil or moral, we become instantly *guilty* by *free will*, and thereby incur a demand for punishment. In religious matters, that punishment may be as severe as condemnation to hell (a place of constant torment) forever. In civil matters, a major breech, such a murder may incur the death penalty. In both of these, the punishment is in the form of pain; one, burning in hell forever; the other forfeiting one's life.

Observing and understanding the source of those remedies, demonstrates clearly the total lack of understanding or concern for the lives and feelings of those less fortunate. As a society, we must recognize that we all live in "glass houses". As such, we must alter our thinking from an automatic stance of *punishment to a more rational attitude of rehabilitation.*

As a society, we must have laws (norms of activity) by which we live and function. When we breech those laws, corrective measures are mandated and justified. If someone is a habitual thief or murderer, he/she must be removed from society until and if such time as he/she can be reliably rehabilitated (redirected down the correct path of thinking). I am thoroughly aware that each of us has been inculcated with the attitude of revenge when we have been wronged. More correctly, however, our attitude should be one of *sorrow and remorse* for the wrongdoer rather than *revenge and pity* for ourselves.

Our entire legalistic attitude comes from the false notion of "free will". There is no such thing. The will does exactly what the intellect tells it to do, and that is always what the intellect perceives as better. Because of misdirected personality programing, so-called criminals see as desirable (good) what society has determined to be unacceptable (bad). Before we as a society can thrive in a meaningful, enriched, loving way, that fact must be recognized, honored and addressed. We need to be spending our resources, in the first instance, in assisting, in whatever way possible, acceptable personality development, and, in the second instance, in promoting reprograming and rehabilitation of criminals. It would be a completely utopian idea to suggest that all could be rehabilitated, but I believe sufficient numbers could be achieved to justify and mandate such programs.

In the absence of such efforts, I see a rapid decline of civilized society in our nation and worldwide at an alarming pace. Anarchy will prevail and civilization will fail. Even as I write, we have a near such situation in Washington D.C. where those who believe and promote the idea that, *anything goes,* just to get votes versus those who believe that *nothing goes.* There is total impasse because, seemingly, neither side understands the problem or worse yet, seems to care.

The *answer* is simple; *its application*, extremely complicated. We must expose our children to societally acceptable behavior based on love of God and neighbor, rather than fear of reprisal with threats of hell and/or gas chamber. That's a very tall order because of the breakdown of the family unit. When the family unit fails, very likely the system fails.

So, in summary, our society has been programed with the Judea-Christian idea for justice; i.e. "eye for eye-----". To use an old but never trite expression regarding these matters; "WHAT WOULD JESUS SAY?". I know what He supposedly did say;" -love your neighbor; do *good* to those who hurt you---".

CHAPTER 29

On Magisterium

THE TERM ITSELF, AS USED by the church, implies an absolute teaching authority to the point of excommunication and or condemnation to hell for non-adherents. In earlier days when the pope was basically the supreme ruler of the world, heretics would be exiled, tortured, or executed ostensibly for protection of the faith. If we are to believe anything at all about Jesus, it would be his basic non-bellicose nature. His teachings were to *love your neighbor, be kind to those who hate (hurt) you*. I don't accept that Jesus would have ever suggested or condoned those activities of the church under the guise of magisterium. Many examples of church abuse of power in opposition to Jesus' position exist but I will mention a few to elucidate the point.

1. The execution or exile of any heretic following 1st council of Nicaea in 325. Granted, the church did not perform the execution, but very willingly identified those to be executed or exiled.
2. The church's attitude toward marriage and sex: marriage under any circumstance was considered sinful and was not allowed inside church buildings (it was performed at church door but outside the building). Sex between married partners was at best grudgingly allowed but no pleasure could be derived from the act (it had to be performed in the abstract). There was a time when Thomas Aquinas proclaimed that male masturbation was the greatest sin that could be committed because the male semen contained all the live babies and they would die. Likewise, sex with the woman

on top was prohibited for same reason (all the babies would run back out of woman's vagina and babies would die). It should be noted that during the INQUISITION, these acts were punishable by unbelievable torture and eventual death by various means, but usually by burning at the stake.
3. INQUISITION- volumes could be written but a few glaring examples:
    a. The MALLEUS MALEFICARIUM of Heinrich Kramer and Jacob Springer carries the Imprimatur of Pope Innocent VIII. This manual is divided into three sections namely, 1-the fact that witches exist, 2-how witches operate, and 3-the various remedies for dealing with witches. Reportedly, thousands of innocent people were found to be witches, and were tortured severely, and many executed. The Protestants even got into the witch hunt and carried it on even into the new world before its' being outlawed.
    b. Galileo Galilei- the famous scientist, astronomer, who discovered the solar system and described its organization and activities in writing, was force to recant his discoveries in public in order to escape execution by the inquisition. The official position of church was that the earth was the center of the universe and Galileo's assertion of the sun being the center was pure heresy and punishable by death. In spite of his recanting, Galileo was forced into house arrest where he lived his last 9 years. During that time, he laid the groundwork for the physical laws of a falling object, later defined by Sir Isaac Newton.
4. The terrorizing of the faithful by church laws: I was taught that a breach of any church law was a mortal sin punishable by immediate condemnation to hell if one died before confessing the sin. Very few of these laws and regulations have been eliminated. However, the fact that many of these laws, particularly attending mass on Sundays and Holy days, and laws regarding sex and birth control, have been largely ignored, has prompted Pope Francis to advise

the world wide clergy to *quit talking about them.* I'm assuming the purpose of his proclamation is to halt the alienation of the faithful. The reason seems obvious; whether or not people sin is unimportant, but the money they contribute definitely is.

5. The Crusades: those wars waged under direct orders from the pope and some of which were led by the pope himself, were in direct opposition to Jesus' teachings. I'm not aware of any Jesus reference for justification of an invasive war. A preemptive strike or war would be justified in self-defense, but the crusades were waged ostensibly to win back the Holy Land.

My contention then is that the church abdicated its' right to magisterium centuries ago. The church, like any organization has every right to make its' rules of membership, *but it does not have the right of dictatorship over our immortal souls.* Ostensibly the Church has ignored that fact and, consequently, has never been in sync with Jesus.

CHAPTER 30

Human Nature and Social Experiment

§

THROUGHOUT HISTORY MANKIND HAD TRIED various social experiments of government, and witnessed the total collapse and failure of each as it evolved, developed, and failed. While I don't proclaim to know the detailed history of every "ism" that ever existed, it is quite obvious that few are in existence today. The reason for the systematic collapse of each has been the failure of the organizers to recognize and address the fundamental evil of humans, namely selfishness and greed. They assumed that a platonic idea of whatever kind would be accepted and honored by the masses; how wrong they were! Let's examine a few.

Feudalism: In this system, a king (lord) ruled over his property. In order to better manage and defend his property and to attain wealth for himself, he employed vassals (governors-generals) whose responsibility it was to see to it that the peasants (slaves) worked hard and produced well, in addition to going to battle to defend the king when he was threatened. The vassals were reasonably well compensated but the commoners were not. Eventually Homo sapiens rebelled and gradually the system was eliminated. People will not be oppressed forever.

Theocracy (church state): The most notable example in modern history is The Holy Roman Empire under Constantine The Great. When government tries to impose religious rule on society, it is doomed to failure because of lack of internal support. Not enough people are willing to believe what is being chocked down their throats, and when outside forces threaten, they will not defend against them. Constantine's empire collapsed eventually. In near modem times, we are witnessing right before our eyes the constant unrest and resistance in the theocratic Islamic states.

Socialism-Communism: Here we have similar conditions whereby the state basically owns everything. The people work for the state and the benevolent state redistributes to the people. If man were perfect, this system would work perfectly. However, man is selfish, greedy, and lazy. Therefore, many fail to produce as expected and desired, yet expect to share equally or more. This, of course, results in a deficit production with resultant diminished distribution of goods and services until such time as economic and or military disaster force collapse of the system; recent examples Mussolini 's Italy and Stalin's USSR. At this very moment we are witnessing near collapse of almost all of Europe because of extreme socialistic trends. Those so-called democracies have failed to install the proper safeguards against too much entitlement, to the point that the populace have grown to expect everything for nothing; most rational and honest people know there is no such thing as a *free lunch*.

It is true that a few communist governments still exist. North Korea, which seems desperate and destitute, could continue to exist only with major support from China. Castro's Cuba, by his own recent admission was a terrible ideological mistake. That admission coupled with his statement that he wouldn't do it again, leads me to believe that their system is near collapse. Communist China is thriving but only because they have exploded onto the capitalistic scene with vigor. I don't expect immediate conversion to democracy, but it seems evident that more and more of their populace are enjoying the western lifestyle. That will eventually lead to an internal collapse of communism or at least a gradually accelerating conversion to democracy.

Democratic Capitalism: Under that system, each citizen can expect the opportunity for life, liberty, and pursuit of happiness. It is expected that every individual has the right to work for his own gain, to own his own property, and have protection provided by his central government. Social and economic norms will be established and honored at the local level. It is expected that certain services which transcend local boundaries, and are for the common good of all will be provided by the central government. That, of course, requires that each person help support those causes in the form of taxation. Our officials are, for the most part, elected to represent the interests of their local constituents. In addition they legislate for the common good of the entire nation. We have a constitutional government which is administered by a president and his cabinet, legislated by a congress, and adjudicated by a court system up to a supreme court. Our founding fathers, recognizing the inherent selfishness and greed, as well as laziness in people, instituted that government in the belief that, given an opportunity, most people would be productive. To date that seems validated. Our system affords checks and balances in order to curb unconstrained greed, and in some degree to make laziness distasteful. We have a multi-party system of government which, depending on party power shifts, causes the economic and social pendulum to swing from the more liberal to the more conservative sides. The utopian spot would be complete pendulum standstill in total equilibrium. In the *real* world, with very selfish, greedy and lazy people, that equilibrium is not likely to ever be achieved.

Nonetheless, our system of government, while experimental in its origin, has proven to be the most dynamic and successful the world has ever known. It is not perfect by our standards, but it is perfect for what it is.

CHAPTER 31
The Future of Christianity

THE HISTORY OF CHRISTIANITY IS **extremely** difficult to discern and therefore precarious to discuss. That is especially true of the so-called, apostolic period (roughly 33 AD until 100 AD), the post apostolic period and the pre-Nicene period. I have done extensive research about beliefs, and practices during that early church "history", and it seems references to recorded history are few. More importantly, it is noticeable that each commentator has a personal bias about what early writers actually said and meant. There does seem to be general agreement on a few things. They are as follows; 1- earliest followers of Jesus held the "breaking of the bread" ceremony in individual homes. 2-by the time of John's death, the "transfer of power", that is the establishment of a hierarchy, was already in place. The most prominent male citizen in each community was consecrated Bishop; he was the sole ruler in his domain and presided at all baptisms and at most agape (breaking of the bread) meals. Although there was a pope, he did not appear to have any particular universal pastoral authority and the Bishop of Rome frequently disagreed with Bishops of the Eastern Church; some seemed to be doctrinal differences, others seemed to be authoritative.

It is generally taught and believed that Peter was the first pope and the first bishop of Rome. However, Garry Wills in his book "What Paul Meant" chronicled Paul's writings and shows that Peter never set foot in Rome; he was killed some 20-30 miles outside Rome before he ever reached the city. Be that as it may, Paul never agreed with Peter and James about who Jesus was nor how salvation was to be attained. Needless to say, by the time of John's death, roughly AD 100 there was mass confusion about how Christian observance was to be conducted, where, and by whom.

Many writers show the agape meal was celebrated in individual homes. In the post-apostolic period, some writer ascribe this meal as being celebrated by the bishop in a specified place. Some references describe a somewhat different discipline regarding baptism and "breaking of the bread "ceremony.

There were many heresies or heretical versions of Jesus assumed teachings. Two, of the most notable, were Gnosticism and Arianism. Gnosticism apparently existed before Jesus teachings appeared, but were incorporated into different forms of Christianity after the first Century. Historically, there seems to have been various versions. One such segment believed that all natural creation was corrupt and evil, and, therefore, no evil act was consequential. Others believed self- restraint was beneficial. Most all believed that all supernatural spirits were good. For further information about those sect(s), please refer to Gnostic writings. The Arians, on the other hand, believed that Jesus was the Son of God but not His equal. Some of the first Nicene Council members were Arian bishops.

Needless to say, by the time Constantine convened the 1st Council of Nicaea, 325 AD, there appeared to be mass confusion and sometimes violent disagreement about many things. Most seemed to be concerned with Jesus' identity, His relationship with God, His second coming, the Eucharist, and much more. The Pauline, Petrine, and Eastern philosophies were at odds over practically every aspect of Jesus devotion .There was not only verbal bickering, but physical hostilities occurring on a regular basis, so any attempt at establishing a true physical and spiritual hierarchy in the Jesus movement met with little success.

At the same time, and for 300 plus years prior, the official state religion of the Roman Empire was Mithraism. That was a pagan religion whereby penitents' "sins" could be abolished by allowing the blood of a freshly slaughtered bull to spill through the cracks of an elevated platform onto them with resultant spiritual cleansing. The bull would be led up onto the platform, and while the penitents stood below the platform, the Mithra (priest) slaughtered the bull allowing its' blood to spill through the cracks onto penitents below. Throughout history, many have claimed Catholic doctrine to have been derived thusly; those claims have been vigorously disclaimed by the Catholic Church; I'm not certain of how convincingly. Historically, Mithraism became official Roman State religion about BC 60-10 and remained so until 1st Council of Nicaea AD 325.

So summarizing to this point, we have seen a disjointed Jesus movement, perpetuated by various proponents, each with its' own version of who Jesus was and what He represented. By the time Constantine convened the Council at Nicaea, there were many arguing (some warring) factions, each with its' own set of religious literature. Constantine reasoned that his rule would be much easier if his empire had one state religion. Since the Jesus movement was displacing Mithraism at a steady pace, and since the Jesus people were the most difficult to contain and rule, and even though Constantine, himself, was a pagan, he decided to make the Jesus religion (Christianity) the official state religion of the Roman Empire. Accordingly, he convened the 1st Council of Nicaea. There were 1800 bishops in the world at the time, but reportedly only about 280-290 attended. Even though Constantine had offered them free travel, lodging and food expenses, the remainder declined; I have often wondered why. Even the pope did not attend. Constantine's purpose was to solidify Christian doctrine and mandate its' acceptance. Any dissenters had the choice of decapitation or exile. Those attending the council, fashioned a church based on their interpretation of who Jesus was including His specific relationship to God. That required dispelling what they considered to be heresies. Also, they apparently chose some writings as authentic, but not all of the eventual biblical cannons. Their main objective seemed to be the establishment of a creed. The Nicene Creed was only partially formalized at that time and further elaborations were added at later councils. They also established a specific time for celebration of Easter each year. It should be noted that even though only 16-17 percent of known Christian religious authorities attended, Constantine gave that relatively small assembly freedom to fashion a religion of its' own choice. It goes without saying that what emanated from that council can and should, rightly so, be called and accepted as a *man-made religion*. My reasoning mandates the following concept; "if the *apostles and their followers* didn't know what Jesus meant, it certainly was unlikely that a group of bickering antagonists would know 300 years later". In any event, their decisions were what ruled the land. Of course, adjustments in philosophy, theology, and dogma ensued on a regular basis for centuries. Even today, rules, regulations, and recommendations are being extruded from the Vatican at almost the frequency of "machine gun fire".

Things went fairly smoothly until Constantine's death. Eventually, the Holy Roman Empire, as it was known, fell. The Moors invaded Spain; Mohammed was born in Mecca 570; Pope Gregory the Great made major liturgical changes apparently in an attempt to contain and obtain converts. Squabbles continued between the Roman Church and the Eastern Church until finally the Great Schism occurred between Rome and Eastern Orthodoxy in 1054. In the meantime, the Muslims, Egyptians, mid-eastern and North African Monarchies were battling constantly, conquering and loosing territory from mid-east to Portugal. The Holy Land had fallen. In 1096, the 1st crusade was undertaken with many to follow. The Chinese got into the fray for about 200 years. The crusades lasted, intermittently, until 16th century. Some were led by popes themselves. Their sole purpose was to win back the Holy Land.

In the meantime, there were religious denominations springing up everywhere; some with explicit doctrine; others seemingly bastardized. Roman Catholicism was in a constant state of defense, with bad popes; more than one pope at same time etc. In an attempt to suppress heresies, a series of inquisitions were begun, with many innocent people being tortured and burned to death. Intermittently, they lasted in various places about 500 years. After bad popes had squandered the church treasury, it resorted to buying and selling indulgences (a lessened period of time in purgatory). That was just one of the gross moral aberrations created by the church that prompted Martin Luther to break with the Church in 1517. The Protestant Reformation was begun, and the rest is fairly common history, including Henry V111 breaking with Rome over divorce and forming the Church of England.

The Church tortured and killed people in every way imaginable until legal authorities put an end to it in this country in the late 1690's.

So, "fast forward" till now. What do we have? According to the World Christian Encyclopedia, there are 33,000 separate Christian denominations in 238 countries in the world today, each claiming to be the correct version of Christianity. What an alarming number! Even more alarming is the condition which generated such confusion. I maintain that it was a "singular" condition; one, either not known or understood, or one ignored by authorities for selfish purposes. The former, as I have stated many times previously, is the more likely; the apostles simply didn't know who Jesus really was. Even though, they probably all were illiterate in the common usage of the term, they undoubtedly were conversant with the fact that long-standing Jewish verbal tradition emphasized the coming of a messiah who was to reestablish paradise here on earth just for them. Even though Jesus seemed to be sincere, knowledgeable, and understanding of God and His workings, he was not able to convince them of His and God the Father's real nature and association. Neither was he able to disestablish the myth promulgated throughout the centuries of a glorious Messiah who would recreate their long-suffered, awaited, new paradise. They simply couldn't understand what He was telling them about the "real kingdom of God". Neither could they accept his attempts at dispelling the historical myth they had been taught. So when Jesus was killed, all sorts of stories began to flourish about Him; to date, they have not ceased.

There are unproven assertions that the only apostle who truly understood Jesus' message was Judas. It has been claimed in the so-called "Gospel of Judas" that Judas was Jesus confidant, and that *the betrayal* was planned by Jesus. In which case, Judas' suicide, if it really happened, would most likely have been precipitated by sadness and despair from the loss of his closest friend.

Pure logic demands that only one of the 33,000 denominational beliefs in existence can possibly be true; more importantly, implied logic suggest the probability that none is true. Accepting those premises as true, one would be compelled to ask the simple question "why"? Believe it or not, the answer is crystal clear. No one, except possibly Judas, knew who Jesus was, and more importantly, seemingly didn't want to know. John seemed to have an inkling of Jesus' message.

The Jews were expecting a glorious Messiah to come swooping in like a giant eagle. He would instantly rearrange and reorganize the earth into a glorious kingdom (paradise), just for them. Everyone would live in perpetual peace and comfort. When Jesus told them the factual truth, they were bewildered; they couldn't conceive of a Messiah coming in the form of a poor carpenter's son. They were completely unable, unwilling, or both, of accepting Jesus as an ordinary human genius, who understood God and his universe; who recognized the universal evil of selfishness created by God in order for His universe to function; who recognized that the image (Will-Spirit) of God was mirrored in all existences, including His own, and since He was the only one to recognize that fact, he had to be the messiah by default; it was his duty to "pay the price of perfect love and perfect justice". His followers simply couldn't accept that. As a result, after His death, all sorts of stories sprouted like freshly sowed wheat. There was no universal understanding or agreement about hardly anything pertaining to Jesus. Guess what? It's still that way and getting worse.

Mind you, this treatise speaks nothing to the other great religions of the world such as *Islam, Buddhism, Hinduism, etc.*

Now the truth:

Jesus was a fully human genius who recognized God's image in everything, including Himself. If we plotted the IQ of every human that ever lived or ever will live on a "bell" distribution curve, we would find Jesus far off the right edge (higher IQ side).

He knew His essence mirrored God's and since both were perfect, they had to accept (love- choose) each other (Holy Spirit).

Through His wisdom, He saw two commanding dictums for happiness; Love God and love neighbor (who is God).

Common rationality teaches us one simple truth which can be stated with different words, but offers the same conclusion. Sallust is credited with saying "harmony makes small things grow; lack of harmony makes great things decay". Our Kentucky state motto "United We Stand; Divided We Fall" is another set of coherent words leading to the same conclusion.

MY HOPE

That the truth of what I have written will eventually be recognized and accepted by thoughtful, philosophical, and spiritually truthful people; that the hoax of organized Christianity will be recognized by the masses; that the truth of the "real Jesus" and His relationship to God and to all His creation will be understood and accepted by most, hopefully all; that people's way of life will automatically be directed by Jesus command that we accept God and our neighbor with fervor; that this understanding and attitude will be the norm in all aspects of our lives; philosophical, interpersonal, educational etc. Selfishness will never be eliminated until we enter eternity, but extreme selfishness, (greed, rape, murder etc.), would and should be reduced to a minimum. For those fewer unfortunate ones, our governmental resources, in the form of appropriate psychiatric care, would be much more available and beneficial. Then, and only then, can we say, "We have a truly caring, sharing, God loving and people loving world".

The "curative" process must start with the major denominations. Once they submitted to the "truth", and demonstrate clearly their acceptance of it, the smaller denominations would rapidly follow suit. Of course, initially, there would be mass opposition and rebellion among the faithful". Their prior brainwashing would require a much different type of "cleanser"; in time most would become spotless. Every rational human being is looking for meaningful guidance; the onus is on the guides, *the Churches*. It's, always embarrassing and painful for a guide to admit he/she is lost, and have to resort to asking for help. However all good, sincere, and honest guides do exactly that. A proud, boastful, egotistical guide will proceed, indiscriminately searching for some sign of a correct path, but invariably becomes more lost in the process. What I see is exactly that; our guides are hopelessly lost, but none will admit it. By doing so, "they would lose everything but their soul"; *Money, Power, Control*. Jesus has already cleansed their souls.

MY PREDICTION

In the absence of the above scenario, and because of lack of understanding and acceptance of the truth of Jesus' real identity, organized Christianity will collapse of its' own weight, and vanish from face of the earth. More and more people bearing down on the literal text of an unreliable book, in a futile attempt at explaining the identity of this real human person with a mythical history, will form more and more Christian denominations. The time will come when literally each household which attempts to cling to some form of Christian identity will be a separate denomination unto itself. By that time, most of course, will have abandoned the idea completely, or will have accepted some other religious identity.

In the absence of the acceptance of my explanation of "the real Jesus", I predict the cults of Christianity will vanish from the face of the earth in the next 100-500 yrs. The length of the extermination period will be dictated, in greatest degree by indirectly unrelated world events; *wars, more wars, and more wars.*

DO YOU SEE WHAT I SEE?

Summary

Any attempt at a comprehensive summary of this writing would be a daunting task to say the least. However I shall try.

1- I was taught Roman Catholic Religion as though it were an exact science for 15 years.
2- When first exposed to the potential perils of sin and sacrilege, I became terrified because it seemed too easy to slip and loose one's soul to eternal damnation forever (a more than terrifying thought).
3- At about age 11-12, I began noticing that nothing I prayed for materialized. That, of course, created not only great consternation but uncontrollable wonderment; what did it all mean? I was told it was the result of God's will. At that time I gradually began to conclude that if I could never change God's mind, then the obvious seem inevitable; God's Will simply was not changeable. All the praying in the world made no difference; nothing changed.
4- It was about that time in my life that I determined that the mythical image and description of God I had been taught was in complete error.
5- With that in mind, I began the process of developing a completely different definitional concept of God. God became as He always had been "A Perfect Rational Being". That definition explained everything. From all eternity God's Intellect and Will were unchanging and unchangeable; can something perfect change? If so it would no longer be perfect.

6- So, from that one simple, singular, concept came all the seemingly impossible answers. Every existence and every occurrence of every existence had been ordained by God's Perfect Intellect and Will from all Eternity and were not subject to any change. What a beautiful realization; "I no longer had to be God's judge".
7- That realization brought questions about eternity; simply put, where there is no change, there is no time; where there is no time, there is only eternity. So God, not possible of change, exists in Eternity.
8- What about His universe which is constantly changing and which He created, and why did he created it that way (totally selfish = evil)? That answer seems clear. If God is Perfect, He must be Perfect Love. Love requires a lover and a lovee. What better lovee could God have than an entire universe of selfishness (evil) which He, Himself created to Love, Accept, Choose AND ABOLISH all stain of evil (selfishness), and, in so doing, become Perfect Love?
9- I failed to mention that the only evil in the universe is *selfishness*; God made it that way so His universe could function. If there were no selfishness, there would be no need; there would be no change nor time; only Eternity.
10- So where does that leave us at this point? Enter Jesus. Jesus was the Einstein of his time. He knew scripture better than the wisest scribes; He recognized, without doubt, the eternal presence of the Spirit of God in everything; nothing could exist without God first imagining it and willing it. Jesus knew that His spirit and the spirit of everything were united in total union with the Father. He also was aware that "The Price had to be paid" before God could be Perfect Love. His singular awareness of that fact made it mandatory for Him to accept the challenge, which He so graciously did: He "paid the ultimate Price" that all creation could be cleansed permanently of its evil (selfishness). That ultimate cleansing occurs only at death.
11- He did so willingly but not without unbelievable human agony (Jesus was human). He knew that His soul and our soul, and the

spirit (soul) of every grain of sand were inexorably imaged with the soul of Almighty God.

12-Jesus willingly but painfully paid the Father's price for Perfection.

13-And what about the Holy Spirit? Simply stated the Holy Spirit (Will of God) (God's Perfect love) represents the constant Love (Acceptance) relationship between God and His entire creation; is it possible for God to reject His Own Perfection? I think not.

14-Jesus, recognizing the folly of the Jews, gave us two simple commandments; Love (Accept) our God with all our heart and Accept our neighbor (who is God) as ourselves.

15-When Constantine The Great gave the church total control over our spiritual lives, he totally destroyed what Jesus had taught us and succeeded in making the world "ONE GIANT CESSPOOL OF NEUROTICISM WITH MAJOR SUICIDAL TGENDENCIES AND WITH MAJOR GUILT TENDENCIES FOREVER; All for power money and control.

16-Here we are 1700 years later and the charade goes on.

17-Consider this; because of organized religion and irrational ideologies, peace in this world is not possible except through overwhelming force promulgated through some benevolent government. So far, that force has been the USA.

18-There is good news; in spite of all the strife the world suffers on a continuing and continual basis; no matter how proud, egotistical, powerful and torturous men may be; no matter how vain, or powerful they may feel, there is one thing for certain; "Jesus has forgiven us ALL". When our selfishness is stripped away at death, what is left is our essence which is a mirror image of God.

19-Our only justifiable prayer is "THANK YOU LORD, GOD, JESUS AND HOLY SPIRIT (WILL OF GOD). AMEN.

20-In the absence of Christianity accepting that philosophy, I predict its' ultimate demise. *Could anything be more disheartening?*

REFERENCES

1. The Bible; New and Old Testaments' many versions including Douay, Confraternity of Christian Doctrine, the New American bible, King James, and many others too numerous to list.

2. The Other Gospels- Ron Cameron- 1982- the Westminster Press Philadelphia

3. A Short history of Nearly Everything- Bill Bryson- 2003- Broadway Books

4. Catechism of the Catholic Church- second edition 1997

5. Introductory Psychology- Alexander A. Schneider, PhD-1953- Rinehart & Company

6. A Synthesis of Human Behavior- Joseph C. Solomon- 1954 Grune and Stratton

7. Robert Frost- American Poet

8. The Malleus Maleficarium of Heinrich Kramer and Jacob Sprenger- 1971- dover Publications, Inc., New York

9. The Theory of Everything- Stephen W. Hawking- 2000- New Millennium Press

10. The Grand Design- Hawking and Mlodinow- 2010- Bantam books

11. Jesus Interrupted- Bart D. Ehrman- 2009- HarperCollins Publishers

12. God's Problem- Bart D. Ehrman- 2008- HarperCollins Publishers

13. Correcting Jesus- Brian Griffith- 2009- Exterminating Angel Press

14. Sex in history- Gordon Rattray Taylor- 1954- The Vanguard Press New York

15. What Paul Meant- Garry Willis- 2006- Viking (The Penguin Group)

16. Summa Theologica 2nd Edition- Thomas Aquinas